Wrapped
IN
CHRIST

365 DEVOTIONS
FROM THE
PAULINE EPISTLES

BRIAN SIMMONS

BroadStreet
P U B L I S H I N G

BroadStreet Publishing® Group, LLC
Savage, Minnesota, USA
BroadStreetPublishing.com

Wrapped in Christ: 365 Devotions from the Pauline Epistles
Copyright © 2022 Brian Simmons

978-1-4245-6368-5 (faux leather)
978-1-4245-6369-2 (e-book)

Stock or custom editions of BroadStreet Publishing titles may be purchased in
bulk for educational, business, ministry, fundraising, or sales promotional use. For
information, please email orders@broadstreetpublishing.com.

Cover and interior by Garborg Design Works | garborgdesign.com

Printed in China

22 23 24 25 26 5 4 3 2 1

Dedication

To all the wonderful pastors and teachers who devoted their lives
to feed the flock of God, this book is affectionately dedicated.

*If anyone is
enfolded into Christ,
he has become an
entirely new person.*

2 CORINTHIANS 5:17

January

Among the Chosen

You are among the chosen ones
who are called to belong to Jesus,
the Anointed One.

ROMANS 1:6

In his letter to the believing church in Rome, Paul wrote to encourage and establish them in their faith. In the same way he encouraged the Roman church, we can be grounded in the gospel of grace that we find within Paul's writings.

The kindness and compassion of God toward us has called us out as his children. We are among the chosen! All who come to faith in Christ have already been called as sons, daughters, and co-heirs with him in his glorious kingdom. May we each find the open door of Christ's invitation to know his love in deeper, truer, and more liberating ways. His glorious grace meets us with generosity as we turn to him. He has all that we need to thrive in his merciful righteousness. What a wonderful King he is and how oh so tender he is with our hearts.

Jesus, thank you for calling me your own. You have drawn me to your heart with tender kindness, and I cannot stay away. Flood me with your tangible goodness as I look to you.

Built Up by Community

Now, this means that when we come together and are side by side, something wonderful will be released. We can expect to be co-encouraged and co-comforted by each other's faith!

ROMANS 1:12

S omething incredibly powerful happens when we gather in the company of those who believe in Jesus and are committed to wholeheartedly following his ways. Even when we are first getting to know other believers, our faith can build each other's confidence. Our testimonies of God's grace in our lives can be the encouragement that we didn't even realize we needed.

There is comfort in being able to share each other's victories and each other's burdens. We were created for community. We were made to lean on each other in hard times and to celebrate one another in our triumphs. Seek out the company of other believers today, and may you find courage and relief there.

Lord, I know that you have called me to know you, not only through the beautiful relationship between your Spirit and my own but through the body of your believers as well. Flood me with your love through others today and help me to be a conduit of your loving courage to them.

Not Ashamed

I refuse to be ashamed of the wonderful message of
God's liberating power unleashed in us through Christ!
For I am thrilled to preach that everyone who believes is saved—
the Jew first, and then people everywhere!

ROMANS 1:16

The message of the cross is the gospel of our Lord Jesus
Christ. The Jewish nation received the promised salvation
message of the Messiah first, and then the rest of the nations
received it as well. Jesus Christ is the Messiah of everyone who
comes to him through faith. Both the outcast and the fortunate
find their home in him.

Can you echo Paul's statement about refusing to be ashamed
of the gospel? Not only is it good news, but it is also the message
of *God's liberating power unleashed in us through Christ*. That is
wonderful news! As you fellowship with the Spirit of Christ today,
may you be infused with the power of his love and grace.

*Christ Jesus, you are the Lord of my life. I submit my heart to you,
and I won't be ashamed of who you are. Your love is better than any
I've known before. Thank you for your free gift of salvation. I am
undone by your mercy.*

Explosive Faith

> This gospel unveils a continual revelation of God's righteousness—a perfect righteousness given to us when we believe. And it moves us from receiving life through faith, to the power of living by faith.
>
> ROMANS 1:17

What would it look like for you to move past simply receiving life and salvation through faith to the power of living by faith, as Paul explains? Are there areas where you are still trying to earn your favor with God? Christ is clear—salvation is through faith alone. And it is through a living relationship with Christ, through fellowship with his Holy Spirit, that we find our true freedom.

We do not need to "do more" to be righteous in God's sight. The Father sees us through the purity and power of Christ's righteousness. We are free in the love of God, and there is more revelation to receive about the kingdom of Christ than we could ever contain. Let your faith lead you in wonder!

Jesus, I want to know your liberating love more in my life so that my faith becomes an expression of a life lived in communion with you. Thank you for being my righteousness!

Extravagant Kindness

Do the riches of his extraordinary kindness make you take him for granted and despise him? Haven't you experienced how kind and understanding he has been to you? Don't mistake his tolerance for acceptance. Do you realize that all the wealth of his extravagant kindness is meant to melt your heart and lead you into repentance?

ROMANS 2:4

There is little else in this world that can rightly compare to the extravagant kindness of God. He is infinitely patient. He does not grow weary of giving us the space and opportunity to accept his mercy. He draws us with loving-kindness, not with threats.

His kindness melts our defenses when we realize how indescribably good, merciful, and powerful he is! His love leads him to extend mercy at every opportunity. When was the last time you considered the incomparable love of Christ that reaches out to you at every moment? Remember his kindness today, for he is full of compassion toward you.

Lord God, thank you for your love that leads me to repentance. I don't want to take it for granted or let the troubles of this world taint my view of you. I draw near, and I ask for your hand of mercy to give me deeper revelations of your kindness.

Continue in Goodness

For those living in constant goodness and doing what pleases him,
seeking an unfading glory and honor and imperishable virtue,
will experience eternal life.

ROMANS 2:7

I n this verse, Paul explains the destiny that awaits those who live for the Lord and seek to do his will. He describes these people as living out what they believe, what Jesus has said to do, with their focus on their heavenly reward.

Doing what pleases God comes from faith. We first believe in Jesus, who is the Anointed One and Messiah. Then we live out of that place of faith, aligning our actions with our values. When this happens, we bring honor to the one who calls us his own. If we want to be sure of eternal life, we must not only pay attention to what we profess with our mouths but also what dwells in our hearts and how it plays out in our lives.

Lord, my heart is yours. The faith I have is from you in the first place. Build up the foundation of my faith, teaching me your ways as I submit to you. I'm so grateful you're not looking for perfection but for willingness to transform. I want to look like you, living a life of loving intention.

Covered in Peace

When we do what pleases God,
we can expect unfading glory,
true honor, and a continual peace—
to the Jew first and also to the non-Jew.

ROMANS 2:10

When we live for what pleases God, the expectations of our hopes are great. Though we will walk through trials and troubles in this life, we can fix our eyes on the prize of our lives— the age that is yet to come in the fullness of Christ's kingdom. We see in part now, but then we will see everything fully. There is unfading glory in our eternal places in his kingdom.

True honor comes from submitting to the Lord and letting him be the final say over our lives. He is kind, patient, powerful, full of love and grace. He is the most loving leader. He is the strongest ally. He is all that we need and so much more than we can imagine. He covers us in his peace even in the midst of our storms. He is with us, steadfast, and good.

Jesus, you are the one I look to today and every day. You are my hope, and I long to please your heart more than any person. Cover me in your glory, honor, and peace.

Heart Circumcision

You are Jewish because of the inward act of spiritual circumcision—
a radical change that lays bare your heart. It's not by the principle
of the written code, but by power of the Holy Spirit.

ROMANS 2:29

The Jewish nation practiced many rituals in line with the law of God, as given through Moses. One such practice is circumcision. In this passage, Paul encourages those who have come to follow Christ by explaining that their salvation and belonging don't come from religious rites but from the power of God at work in their hearts.

This is true for all of us. It is not what we do that makes us pleasing before the Lord. It is the power of his work in us that purifies us. The Holy Spirit radically transforms our hearts as we submit to his hand in our lives. We should all rejoice that this is God's work and not ours. May true confidence and comfort come from the living and active work of God in us and not what we can do for him.

Great God, your power at work in my life is greater than my offerings, and it is my confidence. I humble myself before you and invite you to transform me in even greater ways, doing what only you can do.

He Is Forever Faithful

What if some were unfaithful to their divine calling? Does their unbelief weaken God's faithfulness? Absolutely not! God will always be proven faithful and true to his word, while people are proven to be liars.

ROMANS 3:3–4

We cannot overstate the significance of God's faithfulness being based on his character and not on our belief. God cannot go against his vows. He will never abandon a promise that he has made. That would make him a liar, and we know that God cannot lie. He is not wishy-washy or able to be trapped or manipulated. He is full of clarity, truth, power, and love. He is faithful to his Word!

This should be a relief to our hearts and cause us to rejoice. Our God is faithful, regardless of our unbelief. And yet, there is strength and hope in faith that holds on to the faithfulness of God. Let us not give up believing that he will come through on his promises, for the one who promised is forever faithful.

Faithful Father, I cannot begin to thank you for the wonder of your faithfulness in this world and in my life. I give you my worries and fears, and I invite your peace to bring clarity and calm to my mind and heart. I trust you!

Christ, Our Tangible Righteousness

Now, independently of the law, the righteousness of God is tangible and brought to light through Jesus, the Anointed One…It is God's righteousness made visible through the faithfulness of Jesus Christ.

ROMANS 3:21–22

Christ is the gracious gift of God to a dying world. We could never be righteous enough on our own to earn the favor of God. In fact, God never expected we would. He provided the righteousness of his own Son, Jesus, to be our own. Jesus, the Anointed One, was faithful in life and in death, and he resurrected in the power of the Holy Spirit to once and for all defeat the power of sin and death over us all.

It is in Christ alone that we find salvation. He came to set the sinner free, to heal the sick, and to show us the way to the Father. He is our heavenly door, the one we enter through to the throne room of heaven. He is our righteousness, and in him, we are purified, liberated, and accepted. What wonderful news!

Jesus, thank you for being the salvation and righteousness of all those who come to you for shelter. You are my hiding place. Love me to life in your presence as I realize the powerful purifying mercy of your heart toward me!

Waterfalls of Favor

Through his powerful declaration of acquittal, God freely gives away his righteousness. His gift of love and favor now cascades over us, all because Jesus, the Anointed One, has liberated us from the guilt, punishment, and power of sin!

ROMANS 3:24

P aul makes it clear that God's justice is not separate from his mercy and grace. Jesus Christ is our Redeemer. He has taken the weight of our sin and shame, and he has set us free to live in the light of his own righteousness. His loving favor washes over us in the same measure that it cascades over Christ, for we are found in him.

Are you living in the freedom of Christ? Have you found your liberation in his love? There is no substitute for the gracious favor he grants all those who come to hide themselves in him. Align your life with him, and you will find the relief, rest, and freedom you've been longing for.

Jesus, you are my liberator! I run to you and hide myself in your love. Wash over me with the generous flow of your mercy-tide. Continually transform me in your loving-kindness, for I am yours.

Standing on Christ

There was only one possible way for God to give away his righteousness and still be true to both his justice and his mercy— to offer up his own Son. So now, because we stand on the faithfulness of Jesus, God declares us righteous in his eyes!

ROMANS 3:26

Wherever we find ourselves today, may we be aware of the firm foundation of Christ's faithfulness upholding our very lives. When we stand on his work, we do not need to rely on ourselves. He is our rock-steady ground. He is our salvation, and we will never find another.

We are not saved by grace only to strive again. We have been saved by grace through faith in Christ alone as our Redeemer. His work is finished, and we come alive in his life within us through fellowship with the Holy Spirit. No matter the state of the world, God is faithful. No matter how hard the days are that we are living in, Christ is still moving to set captives free and to fulfill his Word on the earth.

Christ, you are the foundation I have built my life upon. I will not be moved by shifting ideologies or the winds of the world. I am alive in you, and you won't let me go! Thank you.

Faith Counted as Righteousness

No one earns God's righteousness. It can only be transferred when we no longer rely on our own works, but believe in the one who powerfully declares the ungodly to be righteous in his eyes. It is faith that transfers God's righteousness into your account!

ROMANS 4:5

Nothing we do could ever earn us God's favor. Though there is good that we can and should do in our lives, that is not the basis for how we are received by the Father. Jesus Christ alone is our righteousness. It is his work that transforms our hearts. May faith in his love, in his mercy, and in his power to save be the basis of our confidence.

Just as nothing we do can garner us favor, no mistakes we make can take away the power of his mercy in our lives either. Though we cannot escape the consequences of our actions, we should never call into question the love of God toward us. Christ will not withdraw his kindness from a repentant heart. Psalm 103:12 says, "Farther than from a sunrise to a sunset—that's how far you've removed our guilt from us."

Lord Jesus, thank you for the promise of your righteousness that breaks the power of shame in my life. I am grateful for the strength of your love!

God's Work Is Enough

Even King David himself speaks to us regarding the complete wholeness that comes inside a person when God's powerful declaration of righteousness is heard over our life. Apart from our works, God's work is enough.

ROMANS 4:6

God's work is enough. Sometimes we need to hear a phrase multiple times for its truth to really sink in. There is nothing we can add to or take away from the work of Christ. It is complete. It is whole. It is enough. Right here and now, it is enough.

The powerful declaration of righteousness rings over the lives of those who look to the Lord. He answers those who cry out to him. He covers them with the liquid love of his presence. He declares them blameless in his sight. He sings songs of freedom over their hearts and minds. Submit to him and find that God's work is enough for you today.

Lord God, thank you for the incredible truth of your sufficiency and power in my life. Thank you for covering me with your confident kindness. Thank you for your mercy that transforms my heart and my hopes! I love you.

Take God at His Word

Against all odds, when it looked hopeless, Abraham believed the promise and expected God to fulfill it. He took God at his word, and as a result he became the father of many nations.

ROMANS 4:18

P aul has already established that God's faithfulness is not dependent on our faith in him. And yet, he goes a step further and explains how faith benefits us. Abraham received a promise from the Lord that did not seem at all probable, but he believed God and took him at his word. He expected God to fulfill the promise.

When the odds are stacked against you and when things seem hopeless, don't let go of the promises of God over your life. Don't give up your faith. The one who has watched over you, who called you forth from the womb, is faithful. He will not let you down. Let faith replace your discouragement and remember who God is! He is faithful and true, and he will never, ever change.

Faithful Father, I need this reminder more than I would like to admit. I believe that you are faithful. I look at your Word, and I remember the testimony of those who have walked with you. You are a God who doesn't go back on your promises. I believe you.

Embrace Jesus

When we believe and embrace the one who brought our Lord Jesus back to life, perfect righteousness will be credited to our account as well.

ROMANS 4:24

Faith is empowering. It leads us not only in our belief but also in our choices. We don't play small to fear when we believe that God will do what he said he would. May we be like Abraham, who was empowered by faith to continue to glorify God.

In the following verse Paul goes on to say, "Jesus was handed over to be crucified for the forgiveness of our sins and was raised back to life to prove that he had made us right with God" (v. 25). It is Christ's sacrifice and the power of his resurrection that fill us with life, hope, and expectation. Let's throw off all that hinders us and believe in the one who brought Christ back to life. The perfect righteousness of God Christ is then our own. Hallelujah!

Jesus, I embrace you, the Father, and the Spirit. Just as you are three-in-one, I find all the parts of myself completely whole in you. Thank you for your overcoming life that fills my own. I believe that I will know your goodness more and more as I follow you and your kingdom ways.

Flawless before God

Our faith in Jesus transfers God's righteousness to us and he now declares us flawless in his eyes. This means we can now enjoy true and lasting peace with God, all because of what our Lord Jesus, the Anointed One, has done for us.

ROMANS 5:1

The gift of God's grace is a beautiful expression of the unconditional love that the Father has toward us. It is not by works that we are saved but through grace. It is the gift of God not earned by the work of our hands. We have been declared flawless before God when we align our lives with Christ. Faith leads us to freedom. What a beautiful and wondrous exchange.

Peace with God is not something that we need to fight for. Rather, it is something that we acquire through surrender. May you find the peace that passes all understanding rises to meet you, surrounds you with comfort, and settles your heart as you look to Jesus, the author of your faith.

Lord Jesus, I find true comfort, peace, joy, and love in you. You wrap around me with the peace of your presence, and your Spirit fills my heart with hope. Thank you!

Joyful Confidence

That's not all! Even in times of trouble we have a joyful confidence, knowing that our pressures will develop in us patient endurance.

ROMANS 5:3

When times of trouble come, they test our trust. What causes our faith to falter, and what causes it to thrive? We cannot escape the trials of life. We each will experience loss, grief, and pain. There is no way out of it. And yet, is our faith dependent on our circumstances? According to Paul, by no means.

There is a joyful confidence that supersedes our circumstances. The pressures of life that happen to us without our input or control can serve as our great teachers. When we feel as if our trials are breaking us open, we have an invitation to expand in our understanding and trust in God. His faithfulness is sure, and we can partner with faith and hope, holding on to him even as he holds on to us.

Christ Jesus, you are the Lord of my life. When my world is turned upside down, I will continue to trust in you. The ease and comfort of my life does not reflect your favor. Your presence is enough to help me through every hardship. I trust you!

Overflowing with Joy

Even more than that, we overflow with triumphant joy in our new relationship of living reconciled to God—all because of Jesus Christ!

ROMANS 5:11

Where is your greatest joy in life? Is it found in the relationships you have or the hard-earned role you have achieved? Even our greatest natural joys and celebrations pale in comparison to the greatness of knowing God through Christ. In all our success, we could never reconcile ourselves to God.

The beautiful and groundbreaking news, though, is that we don't have to. God has already provided a way through Jesus for us to be fully reconciled to God. We have peace with him, not only being fully known by him, but also knowing him in spirit and in truth. There is now nothing that separates us from the love of God in Christ! What a reason to overflow with joy!

Jesus, thank you for redeeming my life, for setting my feet on the firm foundation of your love, and for calling me into your kingdom as your own. I cannot hold back my overwhelming gratitude toward you today! Thank you for the gift of your grace. I am yours, and I come alive in you.

Gripped by Grace

Now, how much more are we held in the grip of grace and continue reigning as kings in life, enjoying our regal freedom through the gift of perfect righteousness in the one and only Jesus, the Messiah!

ROMANS 5:17

R ight here and now, in the midst of our mundane lives, we can find an abundance of grace. The glorious gift of grace is ours no matter the struggles we are facing. We have liberty in the love of our God through Christ!

Are there any areas of your old life that keep you stuck in cycles you want to break free from? The grace of God is available to you. It is sufficient to break the curse of sin's hold. Jesus says in John 8:36, "So if the Son sets you free from sin, then become a true son and be unquestionably free!" Paul also says in 2 Corinthians 3 that wherever the Holy Spirit is, there is freedom. You have the Spirit of God with you, and he is your freedom and righteousness.

Lord, thank you for gripping me with your grace in every moment. Set me free from the lies of shame, fear, sin, and death. I want to live in the light of your face all the days of my life. Shine on me!

Set Free from Sin

> We were co-crucified with him to dismantle the stronghold of sin within us, so that we would not continue to live one moment longer submitted to sin's power.
>
> ROMANS 6:6

Christ's Word over our lives is the final word. When he declares us free from the law of sin and death, we are free indeed. When we continue to live under old mentalities of shame, fear, and doubt, we are not standing fully on the faith of his overwhelming mercy in our lives. It is to our detriment, not to his, when we remain stuck in old ways of thinking and living.

The power of God is stronger than the grave. His love broke the hold of sin and death. It can certainly break the hold that fear has had over our lives. His love is expansive whereas fear keeps us small and controlled. May we live in the fullness of our liberty rather than playing small in cycles that no longer serve us. His ways are always better.

Jesus, it is because of your power in my life that I can live without sin's hold keeping me stuck. As I come alive in your love, I am awakened to the freedom of your grace at work in my life. Thank you!

Filled Up

If we were co-crucified with the Anointed One,
we know that we will also share in the fullness of his life.

ROMANS 6:8

When we align our lives in Christ and when we join our hearts to his, we allow for his power to rearrange our mindsets, expectations, and values. If we claim to follow the Lord Jesus and to live for his kingdom, then our lives will reflect it. When our values reveal the kingdom of Christ and the fruit of his life within our choices, we are sharing in his fullness.

Let's live for God's pleasure, not simply for our own. When we only live to satisfy our desires, the satisfaction is quick and fleeting. When we live for the desires of God at work within us, we are storing up a heavenly reward that nothing can destroy. Let us move, then, in his compassion, and let us live with his love dripping from everything we do.

God, just as you resurrected Christ from the grave, I believe that I, too, will experience the resurrection of life in your kingdom. While I get a glimpse through fellowship with your Spirit, the promised hope of Christ's return to rule and to reign, on earth as it is in heaven, is what I look forward to.

Conquered by Christ

Remember this: sin will not conquer you, for God already has! You are not governed by law but governed by the reign of the grace of God.

ROMANS 6:14

What a gloriously gracious gift God has given us through the life, death, resurrection, and fellowship of his Son, Jesus. Sin is no longer our master, for Christ is. God has conquered our old selves, and sin no longer has the hold on us that it once did.

Though laws keep people in line, they do not liberate. They are the boundaries for a civil life. No one is perfect in keeping God's law—not one person! Perfection was never the goal, and God knew it wasn't possible. He sent his Son to direct us to his kingdom, to be the go-between and our forever High Priest. We are governed by the reign of the grace of God, and that is overwhelmingly good news for all humanity.

Christ, your love has conquered me. You are the leader of my life, and I submit to you. Thank you for grace that governs me, not the letter of the law or standards of perfectionism. I am free to follow your pathway of love, and I won't stop.

Joyous Freedom

As God's loving servants, you live in joyous freedom from the power of sin. So consider the benefits you now enjoy—you are brought deeper into the experience of true holiness that ends with eternal life!

ROMANS 6:22

Living under the grace of God is not a chore, and it is not boring. There is incredible freedom, overwhelming joy, and satisfying peace in being free from the demands of sin. We now enjoy many benefits of grace, and grace leads us into deeper holiness, not away from it. The righteousness of God as our own is an open door into the liberty of his love.

When Christ's values become our own, we stop living only to satisfy ourselves. Our worlds expand in his mercy and compassion. Our mindsets are transformed to think about others as much, if not more than, we are concerned with our own comfort. His love is ever reaching, and as we are moved by it, we will find that we, too, reach outside of ourselves to extend his kindness to others.

Yahweh, you have set me free, and I am filled with joy in your presence. I find that the more liberated I become from my old ways of thinking, the more grounded I am in your love. Thank you!

Fresh New Life

Now that we have been fully released from the power of the law,
we are dead to what once controlled us…now we may serve God
by living in the freshness of a new life in the power of the Holy Spirit.

ROMANS 7:6

H ow empowered do you feel in your life? Do you live in the freshness of new life that Paul is speaking of here? Do you know the incomparable goodness of the power of the Holy Spirit in your life? He moves in subtle ways and in grand gestures. The softening of your heart to another in compassion is as much his work as is the healing of a body.

May you be encouraged to look for how that mercy meets you in little and big ways. Fellowship with the Spirit is your right as a child of the living God. He is near, moving, and always ready to help you. Don't hold anything back today as you pour your heart out to God. Refreshment awaits you in his presence today.

Holy Spirit, fill me with fresh insights, revelations, and encounters with your Spirit. Awaken my heart, mind, and understanding to your living love. Show me your power at work in my life and give me eyes to see.

Renewed by Righteousness

I give all my thanks to God, for his mighty power has finally provided a way out through our Lord Jesus, the Anointed One! So if left to myself, the flesh is aligned with the law of sin, but now my renewed mind is fixed on and submitted to God's righteous principles.

ROMANS 7:25

God has given us renewed minds in his Spirit. We are not left to our own, dependent on our old ways of thinking and understanding. His Spirit's life within us transforms our minds. Life, love, peace, clarity, joy, and so much more grow in his fellowship.

Fix your mind on God's righteous principles today. May you find renewed hope as you submit to Christ's ways above your own understanding. Spend time in the gospels and in the teachings of Jesus. He is full of life-giving wisdom to direct our hearts. Spend time with the Spirit through prayer and meditation. Look to the Lord, and you will find his help. He is so much better than we could ever give him credit for.

Anointed One, your mighty power at work in my life is unrivaled. No one else loves me the way that you do—so purely and without hidden motive! I yield my heart to you. Renew and refresh me in your presence again.

No More Condemnation

So now the case is closed. There remains no accusing voice of condemnation against those who are joined in life-union with Jesus, the Anointed One.

ROMANS 8:1

What once condemned us—namely the law and our inability to abide by the letter—has led us to our saving grace. Christ provided a way out of the curse that loomed over us. We do not need to sacrifice animals in order to feel better about our shortcomings. God does not require anything more from us. Jesus Christ is our salvation, our peace, and our hope.

Is there any area of your life where condemnation's voice is still heard regularly? Be encouraged to take it before the Lord today. What he does not hold against you, you need not hold against yourself. What Christ has liberated you from does not have a claim to you. Simply join your life with his and rest in the confidence of his faithfulness and truth.

Anointed Christ, thank you for the truth of your saving grace breaking the hold of sin over my life. Where I have believed the condemning lies of the enemy, I now yield to you and stand upon the finished work of your cross. I am free in your love—unquestionably free!

Spirit of Life

The "law" of the Spirit of life flowing through the anointing of Jesus
has liberated us from the "law" of sin and death.

ROMANS 8:2

The Spirit of life is flowing through the anointing of Jesus even now. It is accessible to you and me through his Spirit. His liberating love is as available today as it ever was or will be. The Spirit provides fullness of salvation, of peace, of joy, of hope, and of love. The kingdom of Christ sees no lack, no shortage of goodness.

Is there an area of your life that needs a fresh touch from the Spirit? Is there restoration or redemption that you have been longing for? Look to him, for you will find the fullness of all your hopes and expectations in Christ. He is continually unfolding his kingdom in our lives. There is always more to sustain us, to grow us, and to encourage us. May your heart find encouragement in his fellowship today!

Lord God, thank you for your Spirit of life that sets me free from the law of sin and death. I am not confined by my mistakes. I am defined by your righteousness. Thank you! As long as I have breath, I will thank you.

The Anointed Life

Now every righteous requirement of the law can be fulfilled through the Anointed One living his life in us. And we are free to live, not according to our flesh, but by the dynamic power of the Holy Spirit!

ROMANS 8:4

The life of Jesus in us is enough to satisfy God! The dynamic power of the Holy Spirit is released in us, empowering our new life in him. All that we need originates and is found in him.

An anointed life does not begin with what we offer. It begins with receiving. God requires nothing from us. Yes, we submit to and believe in him, but that does not earn our way into his kingdom. We receive the gift of grace, and from that place, we rise as new creations in Christ. We live with the freedom and confidence of his finished work being enough, once and for all! We partner with his purposes not because he needs us to but because it is our privilege to do so. We offer our lives as gifts of gratitude right back to the giver of all good gifts.

Anointed One, I am undone by the power of your love in my life. Move, and I will move with you. Transform me in your mercy, and I will never be the same.

Fully Accepted

Now Christ lives his life in you! And even though your body may be dead because of the effects of sin, his life-giving Spirit imparts life to you because you are fully accepted by God.

ROMANS 8:10

The breath of the Spirit renews and rejuvenates us in our innermost being. It brings life. Though we experience the decay that comes with living in an imperfect world, even in our bodies, our souls are alive in Christ and continually being made new as we fellowship with his Spirit.

Through Christ, God has fully accepted us. Nothing can convince him to withhold his love for us. He will not withdraw the power of his Spirit from moving in our lives. He will not change his mind about transforming us into his image. Let's keep yielding to him, looking to him, and seeking to live according to his kingdom rather than the ways of this world.

Father, thank you for the power of the Spirit in my life. Thank you for the life of Christ, alive in me. Continually transform me by your love. I am yours.

Beloved Child

The Holy Spirit makes God's fatherhood real to us as he whispers into our innermost being, "You are God's beloved child!"

ROMANS 8:16

Paul says in Romans 8:15, "You did not receive the 'spirit of religious duty,' leading you back into the fear of never being good enough." If you had a parent who expected perfection from you, then you know what it is to live as a constant disappointment. Caring parents understand that perfection is out of the question. They offer love, support, care, and correction in the safety of connection.

No matter the earthly parenting you experienced in your own life, God is an exceedingly good Father. He is better than any earthly parent. He is pure in motive, and his kindness doesn't come with restrictions or conditions. Your Father is patient, kind, and full of love toward you. Run into the welcome of his embrace as you meditate on the truth that you are God's beloved child.

Good Father, reveal to my heart in fresh and new ways how deeply your love is toward me. I need a reminder of your goodness. Thank you for revealing yourself through your Spirit in the depths of my soul.

February

Glorious Hope

I am convinced that any suffering we endure
is less than nothing compared to the magnitude of glory
that is about to be unveiled within us.

ROMANS 8:18

Even when we walk through suffering in this life, a promised glory reveals itself through God's Spirit with us. All creation groans, as Paul goes on to say in verses 21–22, in longing for "the wonderful freedom coming to God's children."

The Spirit of God empowers us now in our weakness, giving language to our prayers and interceding on our behalf. The fruit of God's Spirit grows in the garden of our hearts and lives no matter what is going on in the details of our circumstances. When we are yielded to him, his power in us breathes new life, restoration, and hope. While we wait for the fulfillment of every longing in Christ's return, we experience the gracious expansion of his love in our lives.

Spirit, breathe fresh hope into my soul as I look to you. You see my struggles and my challenges, and you are with me in it all. Rise up, Lord, and empower me with your love.

Clear Confidence

So, what does all this mean?
If God has determined to stand with us, tell me,
who then could ever stand against us?

ROMANS 8:31

When we are rooted and grounded in the love of God, chosen to be his very own, knowing our true identity as children of God, our confidence cannot be shaken. With his love as our very foundation, the houses of our lives are built upon his faithfulness.

Are there areas of your life where you feel as if you are standing on shaky ground? Are the winds of testing blowing through and knocking down areas you thought would withstand anything? Take heart and take hope in God your Father. He has not abandoned you, and he will not let you be swept away. When it all comes down, he remains. His love remains. It upholds you and will continue to hold you. Don't fear, for your God is with you.

Jesus, you are the one I cling to in the storms of this life. You are the bedrock of my faith on both sunny and cloudy days. I trust you. I stand with you, Lord, and I ask you to give me eyes to see how you are standing with me.

Unending Love

Who could ever divorce us from the endless love of God's Anointed One? Absolutely no one! For nothing in the universe has the power to diminish his love toward us. Troubles, pressures, and problems are unable to come between us and heaven's love.

ROMANS 8:35

God's love is strong. It is infinitely stronger than we can imagine. When put to the test, it will never fail. Nothing— no persecution, deprivation, danger, or death threat—can get in the way of the generous portion of his love. Nothing can stand in the way of God's mercy offered to us through Christ.

What Christ has done is a final and forever word over sin and death. His sacrifice and his resurrection are our living hope and present power. In Romans 8:37, Paul says, "Even in the midst of all these things, we triumph over them all, for God has made us to be more than conquerors, and his demonstrated love is our glorious victory over everything!" Let that be our daily encouragement, our anchor, and our inspiration.

Christ Jesus, your love is undeterred in my life and in this world. Your love always has the final say. I am more than a conqueror through you, for you are my victory. I believe it.

Rely on His Mercy

Again, this proves that God's choice doesn't depend on how badly someone wants it or tries to earn it, but it depends on God's kindness and mercy.

ROMANS 9:16

I n the preceding verse, Romans 9:15, Paul quotes the Lord when he spoke to Moses: "I will be merciful to whomever I choose and I will show compassion to whomever I wish." It is God's mercy that we grab hold of, not as a beggar reaches for crumbs but as a beloved child seated at his table. We know that our faith does not come from our own works; we cannot earn God's love. He gives it freely.

May you grab hold of the generous mercy God pours over you today. You are not exempt from his promises. He answers all who call on him. He extends unending love toward you. You don't have to be better, strive more, or do anything. Simply receive his kindness. Partake of his goodness. There is more here to taste and see than you have yet known.

Father, I want to know you more than I have before. I want to walk with you in Spirit and in truth, feasting on the truth of your Word. Let your kingdom come in my life as it is in heaven and move in mighty power!

In the Potter's Hand

Who do you think you are to second-guess God? How could a human being molded out of clay say to the one who molded him, "Why in the world did you make me this way?"

ROMANS 9:20

Have you ever struggled to know the confidence of being chosen, wholly loved, and completely accepted? Have you ever second-guessed your worth? When we spend too much time in comparison, which is so easy to do these days in the highlight reels and carefully curated world of social media, we lose sight of what is important.

God made each of us as unique expressions of his creativity. We are living, breathing pieces of art straight from the Potter's hand. Instead of comparing our journeys with that of others, looking to blend into the uniformity of conditioned standards, let's dare to be ourselves bravely. Let's press into the presence of God, the voice of God over our lives, and live out our unique purposes as we pursue his path of love. We are fearfully and wonderfully made.

Lord, thank you for the reminder that I am yours and that I am not a mistake. You made me with my own set of unique talents and quirks. I want to come more alive in you and be wonderfully me, standing on the confidence of your love.

Living Message

God's "living message"...is the revelation of faith for salvation, which is the message that we preach. For if you publicly declare with your mouth that Jesus is Lord and believe in your heart that God raised him from the dead, you will experience salvation.

ROMANS 10:9

Faith is much more powerful than we understand. Faith in Christ as the all-sufficient sacrifice, removing the need for us to perfectly follow the law in order to be saved, is gloriously simple and miraculous. In our humanity, we all fall short of the perfection of Christ. Yet, it is not our own faultlessness that is needed. Christ's love has perfected us, and we receive the purity and abundance of his righteousness.

What wonderful news! The simplicity of the gospel and its message is clear throughout Paul's letters to the early churches. Still, it is as powerful today as it was then. May we each exemplify God's living message and proclaim that Christ is Lord not only with our mouths and our hearts but also with our very lives.

Glorious God, I cannot begin to thank you for the overwhelming goodness of your mercy in my life. I believe that Jesus is Lord, and I will continue to follow you on the path that you have laid out. You are my hope and my salvation.

Never Disappointed

The heart that believes in him receives the gift of the righteousness of God—and then the mouth confesses, resulting in salvation.

ROMANS 10:10

J esus often spoke of the importance of what is hidden in a person's heart. He broke down the law from being outward acts of rebellion to include the attitudes of our hearts. He used the law to reveal how each of us, even if we obey the letter of the law with our actions, cannot excuse the intentions of our hearts when we harbor hate.

In the same way that God can see through our actions, he sees each submission and reach for his love. He sees every sacrifice we make in the name of love, even if no one else does. When we believe in our hearts that Christ is our all-sufficient saving grace, he honors our faith. In Romans 10:11, Paul goes on to quote an uplifting Scripture to encourage his readers, "Everyone who believes in him will never be disappointed." Hallelujah!

Jesus, thank you for being my salvation. Thank you for breaking the curse of sin and death over my life and for leading me into your goodness. Continue to reveal yourself in my life; I won't stop following you.

Promised Renewal

> He has enough treasures to lavish generously
> upon all who call on him…it's true:
> "Everyone who calls on the Lord's name
> will experience new life."
>
> ROMANS 10:12–13

Have you experienced the new life that Paul is referring to here? Have you known the all-surpassing goodness of his powerful presence with you? When you call on the name of the Lord, you will be saved. When you call on Jesus, you have the promise of new life.

In the areas of your life that are longing for renewal, call on the name of the Lord today. Don't hold back your honest prayers from your ever-present help and hope. Ask for his perspective of your situation. Ask for the wisdom of his kingdom to transform your mind. Ask for his help and wait on him. Keep an open line of communication through prayer throughout your day. Lean into his presence and trust him. He will not fail you.

Lord, I open my heart to you and choose to trust that where I am needing revival, you will give it. I look to you for help. You are my hope. I rely on you.

Heart Response

Faith, then, is birthed in a heart that responds
to God's anointed utterance of the Anointed One.

ROMANS 10:17

True faith, as we see Paul describe it, is a response to the revelation of Christ. The Word become flesh, as John puts it. Faith is not based in what we see with our naked eyes, but what we understand in our hearts. The revelation of Jesus as the Son of God, as our Savior, is the power of the gospel.

Have you been transformed by the revelation of Jesus? Has his life imparted renewal and redemption in your own? You have an open invitation every moment to respond to the Lord. God himself is the author of your faith—the originator of it. How will you respond today?

Jesus, I remember what it was like when I first responded in open-hearted faith to your gospel. I recall that moment, that season when I first learned to walk with you. I invite you to do far more, even now, in my willingness. I love you!

Grace-Gifts

When God chooses someone
and graciously imparts gifts to him,
they are never rescinded.

ROMANS 11:29

What God chooses once, he chooses forever. When he invites us to be his children, and we come to him as daughters and sons, he will never turn us away as strangers. What gracious gifts we receive from him! The Spirit fills our lives with the fruit of his kingdom as we surrender to his leadership. He gives us joy, peace, patience, kindness, love, and so much more.

This goes, too, for the calling of God over our lives. At his heart, God is a loving Father who relates to us through intimate fellowship with his Spirit. First and foremost, we are loved by God. He teaches us his wisdom and ways, and he refines us through correction in love. Specific callings will ring true over our lives, but none is as important as the call to love others as we are loved.

Father, I cannot comprehend the lengths of your mercy or the power of your grace. Even so, I will openly look to learn and expand in your revelation-knowledge all the days of my life. Thank you for the gracious gifts you have imparted.

Wonder in the Mystery

Who could ever wrap their minds around the riches of God, the depth of his wisdom, and the marvel of his perfect knowledge? Who could ever explain the wonder of his decisions or search out the mysterious way he carries out his plans?

ROMANS 11:33

Isaiah 55:9 says, "As high as the heavens are above the earth, so my ways and my thoughts are higher than yours." Though our reservoirs of mercy run out, God has an endless supply. Though we are limited in compassion, God is never-ending in loyal love. Neither malice nor manipulation taint his perspective. He sees everything clearly, and in his clarity, he offers the generosity of his mercy and grace.

Even though we cannot comprehend the extent of God's plans or his mysterious ways, let's lean in to know him more. There is always more revelation that leads to increased wonder. Consider how easily awe-struck children are when they experience something for the first time. As we get to know new facets of the Lord and his love, so will we, too, be caught in wonder.

Glorious God, there is no one like you. You are endless in mercy, and you are pure in truth. I want to be caught up in childlike wonder. Reveal yourself to me in new ways as I look to you.

Sustainer of Everything

> Out of him, the sustainer of everything, came everything,
> and now everything finds fulfillment in him.
> May all praise and honor be given to him forever! Amen!
>
> ROMANS 11:36

God is the source of everything. He is even the source of our faith. All that we offer God is a return or a response. We offer back to him what came from him in the first place. God is the Creator of all things, and he is also the Sustainer. May we find encouragement and hope in that truth today.

Everything finds its fulfillment in him, and that includes every hope and longing that we have. Though we taste and see his goodness through many different facets in this life, including our relationships, successes, and service, he is the only perfect representation. He is the perfect Father where ours fall short. He is the lasting love when others come and go. Since, then, we find our satisfaction in him, let's give him praise and honor.

Faithful One, reveal the purity and sufficiency of your love in my life today. I don't want to grasp for straws where I already have all I need. Thank you.

Genuine Expression of Worship

Beloved friends, what should be our proper response to God's marvelous mercies? To surrender yourselves to God to be his sacred, living sacrifices. And live in holiness, experiencing all that delights his heart.

ROMANS 12:1

Our genuine expression of worship is not found in a music service. It is not in singing or dancing. It is in living a life surrendered to the Lord. That is our true offer of pure worship. We give him leadership over our lives, and we move in the wisdom of his love. We follow his voice where he leads, for he is trustworthy. He is our Good Shepherd.

When we live in holiness, we consecrate our hearts and lives to Christ. He is our holiness; he is our covering. Instead of chasing ideals out in the world that constantly shift and change, let's give our energy first and foremost to Christ. He will lead us in love, and he will restore us in his mercy. We can trust him more than any other because he has no hidden motives.

Lord, my life is yours. I want to reflect a heart of gratitude and submission in all that I do. I want to live for your kingdom values above any other.

Inward Reformation

Stop imitating the ideals and opinions of the culture around you, but be inwardly transformed by the Holy Spirit through a total reformation of how you think. This will empower you to discern God's will as you live a beautiful life.

ROMANS 12:2

The world as we know it will come to an end. Our lives are finite, and our experiences of this world are limited. With this in mind, let's fix our eyes on those things that will last forever—our eternal hope in Christ and his coming kingdom.

If our hearts and perspectives are not transformed in the truth of God, then we are missing a key element of what it actually means to be submitted to Christ. Let us not be Christians in name only but with lives that are surrendered to his loving leadership. A beautiful and satisfying life is one that is lived with our focus on the kingdom of God, building on its values here and now. Where there is love, joy, and peace, there is the Spirit of God. Where there is patience, hope, and self-control, the Spirit is working.

Lord, reform and revive my heart, mind, and soul in you. Shift mindsets that have been conditioned by this world and its values in your eternal perspective. Yours is the only wisdom that truly matters.

Joined Together

It is in the body of Christ. For though we are many, we've all been mingled into one body in Christ. This means that we are all vitally joined to one another, with each contributing to the others.

ROMANS 12:5

Every person has his or her own unique gifts and talents. Each one has a purpose and a niche. As the body of Christ, we are not all arms or legs, eyes or hands. Instead of trying to take another's place or role, we can know that there is space for each of us to fill. We do not have to compete with each other; we were meant to be united in love and to support one another.

Have you embraced your own unique function within the body of believers? Or have you been comparing your life, ministry, and opportunities with others? We are not made to do life on our own but with the support, witness, and connection of others. May you find your own part strengthened in the unity of purpose within the body of Christ.

Lord, you are the head of your church, and you are the leader of my life. Thank you for creating me uniquely with a purpose. Build me up in your grace and reflect your glory through the fellowship of your people.

Move in Love

Let the inner movement of your heart always be to love one another, and never play the role of an actor wearing a mask. Despise evil and embrace everything that is good and virtuous.

ROMANS 12:9

How different would your life be if the inner movement of your heart was always to reach out in love to others? How might your relationships change? How might your own perspective shift? Paul encouraged those in the Roman church to check the attitude of their hearts, being sure to align them in the light of God's love.

Love moves in courage, without expectation of a return. It chooses to extend compassion and the benefit of the doubt, while also leaving room for accountability. Love does not put on a show or pretend to be something that it is not. Fill up on the love of Christ, and you will have an overflowing fountain of love to offer others. When you run dry, run to the one who fills your cup.

Loving Lord, I want to be living reflection of your compassion. I want to choose your ways over my own, and I know that means letting down my self-protective mask. I know that there is wisdom in your love, and I choose to follow your path of mercy.

Don't Give Up

Let this hope burst forth within you, releasing a continual joy.
Don't give up in a time of trouble, but commune with God at all times.

ROMANS 12:12

When we are enthusiastic to serve the Lord, radiating with the Holy Spirit, hope will burst forth within us. This hope propels us and sustains us. It releases a continual joy, as Paul says. Even in times of trouble, we can commune with God. We can always fellowship with him, so let's not give up when hard times hit.

The Spirit of God is always available to us. He never abandons us. He is our generously present help in times of trouble, and our provision when we have no resources of our own. He is beyond good. May the hope of Christ be our sustaining grace, and may the power of his presence move us in greater love, joy, peace, patience, and endurance. He will never give up on us, so let's not give up hope! He who began the work within us is faithful to complete it.

Spirit, meet me with the power of your mercy. I want to know the all-surpassing wonder of your presence that fulfills and sustains me. I lean into you, and I ask you to flood me with your peace today. You are my courage.

A Better Word

Speak blessing, not cursing,
over those who reject and persecute you.

ROMANS 12:14

What is your initial response when someone rejects you? Is it to curse them, or do you sink into despair? Rejection is a painful experience, but we should not dehumanize those who do it. Instead of cursing those who curse us, let us bless them, as Jesus taught us to do.

In Matthew 5:44 Jesus says, "Love your enemy, bless the one who curses you, do something wonderful for the one who hates you, and respond to the very ones who persecute you by praying for them." This is not human nature, but it is a value of the kingdom of Christ. We extend love instead of perpetuating hatred. This better word, as given through Jesus and upheld by Paul, is still the standard for those of us in Christ today. Those who chose to walk in his ways receive peace.

Jesus, help me to follow your ways and choose compassion, blessing, and release over the worldly ways of fear and revenge. Give me grace-strength to empower my heart to choose your kingdom values.

Keep Learning to Love

Don't owe anything to anyone, except your outstanding debt
to continually love one another, for the one who learns to love
has fulfilled every requirement of the law.

ROMANS 13:8

As we follow Christ, we will never outgrow his law of love. We will not reach a status in his kingdom that no longer requires a constant expansion in compassion, mercy, and grace. His love is limitless, and so is our opportunity to learn and grow in it.

Love is not selfish. It is also not self-defeating. As we grow in love toward others, we expand in love toward ourselves. We can see the connectedness of humanity in Christ. We can see the reflection of love's image in all creation. So, let's lean into the learning and not give up on continually loving each other, just as Christ has called us to do. More goodness than we can imagine is within this call to love.

Merciful God, thank you for your love that knows no limits. Forgive me for where I have turned a cold shoulder to others instead of letting compassion lead me. Melt my heart in your mercy and move me in your love.

True Fulfillment

Love makes it impossible to harm another,
so love fulfills all that the law requires.
ROMANS 13:10

We've all heard the trope "love is all we need." While some object to this, saying we need justice, truth, and action, perhaps they are not seeing that love is more than a feeling. True love, as reflected in the love of Christ, is evident in the actions that overflow from our hearts. Love is not a fleeting feeling. It is more than a choice. It is the very life-source of creation. It is the make-up of God.

First John 4:7 says, "Those who are loved by God, let his love continually pour from you to one another, because God is love." It is in the pouring out of love to one another that love is evident in our lives. And this is a reflection of God himself. It is impossible to harm others when we value them as highly as we value ourselves. So, let's continually expand and mature in being living images of God's love.

Great God, I want to grow in loving others, even as I come to understand how deeply you love me. May I not get caught up in the excuses to withhold compassion from others when you are inviting me to expand in your mercy.

Full Immersion

Instead fully immerse yourselves into the Lord Jesus,
the Anointed One, and don't waste even a moment's thought
on your former identity to awaken its selfish desires.

ROMANS 13:14

When we put on Christ, clothing ourselves in his person, his identity overtakes our own. It is his royal robes that indicate our true identity. When we are found in him, our old ways pale in comparison. He is full of light, and his light becomes our own shining beacon.

Where have you experienced discouragement in your life? What areas are you struggling to find peace in? May you fully immerse yourself in Christ, taking on the cloak of his righteousness. Picture yourself covering these parts of your life with the royal robes of Christ. Let his power and purity be your covering. Let his resurrection life be the blanket that breeds new life out of barren places. Watch what he does as you do!

Lord Jesus, fill my mind with your perfect peace. Cover my life with your powerful redemption and bring new life out of the ashes of my despair. I look to you.

Open-Handed Welcome

Offer an open hand of fellowship to welcome every true believer, even though their faith may be weak and immature. And refuse to engage in debates with them concerning nothing more than opinions.

ROMANS 14:1

How often do we let our differing opinions lead to divisions between us? In Christ, we should be secure in our freedom but also aware of where other people are coming from. We don't need to argue about our differences and get caught up in them when there is much more that unifies us in the love of Christ and in our humanity.

Have you ever been welcomed into a place with such genuine interest, affection, and care, that it melted your defenses? Let us be those who open our hearts and homes, lovingly offering support to our brothers and sisters in Christ. May it be said of us that we are people who show the love of God through our love of each other.

Father, I don't want to get up in the differences between my opinion and others. It is so hard to resist sometimes! Strengthen me in your grace and help me to lean in with compassion and true hospitality.

Living for Christ

No one lives to himself
and no one dies to himself.

ROMANS 14:7

For those living in fear of how other will perceive their behavioral choices, perhaps there is an invitation in Christ to experience more freedom. For others, they may have no problem living in their freedom, but they may not know how their personal choices are affecting those around them. Living for Christ means finding that balance of living in line with our convictions while also being wise about how we do it.

None of us is an island to ourselves. We are interconnected, and the law of Christ's love is inclusive of this experience. Let us be aware of how our choices may affect those around us while also staying true to our values. We should never use our freedom to thoughtlessly cause another to struggle.

Lord, thank you for the freedom I have in you. I realize that some issues are not black and white, and there is no set right and wrong for every area of life. Help me to lead in love with all I do, and where I fail, may I be quick to repent and repair.

Personal Responsibility

> Therefore, each one must answer for himself
> and give a personal account of his own life before God.
>
> ROMANS 14:12

In the verse leading up to this, Paul quotes from the Old Testament, saying "As surely as I am the Living God, I tell you: 'Every knee will bow before me and every tongue will confess the truth and glorify me!'" (Romans 14:11). The Lord makes it clear that each person is responsible for his or her own choices, in life and in faith. We cannot rely on our family members, friends, or community of faith to skate by.

Do you take agency of your choices? Are you aware of the personal responsibility that is yours over your own life? Surely, a mix of things in life will directly result from choices you make, while other things simply happen to you. Even in the latter, you get to choose how you respond. There is so much grace, so much mercy, so much love available in Christ. But don't forget that only you can account for your life before God.

Jesus, you are my Savior. I realize that life is not simply what happens to me, but I am an active participant. I yield my heart and my life to you.

Walk in Love

Stop being critical and condemning of other believers,
but instead determine to never deliberately cause a brother
or sister to stumble and fall because of your actions.

ROMANS 14:13

When we walk in love, we walk in the light of God. When we follow Christ's commands, we free ourselves up to focus on the things that truly matter and to let go of the things that won't last. Criticism is easily seen these days. Condemnation, on every side, is easy to come by. There is no lack of excuses to shut off our hearts to one another.

Yet, the kingdom of Christ is a kingdom based on mercy and power. It is to our benefit, as well as to the benefit of those around us, to give up our judgmental attitudes and instead live from a place of goodness. If we know that what we are doing is causing a brother or sister to stumble, then we are not walking in the love of the Lord. Love rules our conduct when we live with peace as our priority.

Jesus, I know that your ways are so much better than my own. Where I would choose to deride others' choices, you offer grace upon grace. Fill me with your mercy and empower me as I align my heart, my choices, and my relationships in your love.

Kingdom of the Spirit

For the kingdom of God is not a matter of rules about food and drink, but is in the realm of the Holy Spirit, filled with righteousness, peace, and joy.

ROMANS 14:17

For those of us participating in modern Christianity, we may not fully understand the importance of rituals and rites, abstaining or partaking, depending on the requirements of the feasts and fasts that were written into the Orthodox religious code. However, we may relate to similarities in our own traditions, including whether one should drink alcoholic beverages, when baptism should take place, church music, clothing styles, communion, gender roles, and more.

The kingdom of the Spirit is above the rules and regulations of this world. The kingdom of God is in the realm of the Spirit, where righteousness, peace, and joy are promoted. How do the choices you make, or the judgments you wield, align with this? The kingdom of our God upholds goodness, mercy, and justice, and it does not get caught up on the details that we, as humans, so often do.

Great God, I want to walk in the realm of your Spirit, focusing on the fruits of your work and not the differences in opinion that are so very prevalent. Forgive me for where my focus has been off.

Harmonious Living

Make it your top priority to live a life of peace with harmony in your relationships, eagerly seeking to strengthen and encourage one another.

ROMANS 14:19

How do we live in harmony in our relationships, exactly? In this context, Paul is speaking about the cleanliness of ceremonial foods. Some had the conviction, including Paul, that they could eat anything and be right with God. For others, they felt strongly that they should abstain from certain foods and drink.

In verse 22, Paul says, "Keep the convictions you have about these matters between yourself and God, and don't impose them upon others." *Don't impose them upon others.* We don't have to change our convictions about matters that, in faith, we believe are true. Yet, these areas are not essential issues, and they should not be imposed upon others. This is how we can live a life of peace and harmony with others, seeking to strengthen and encourage one another.

Lord, thank you for the reminder that love takes into consideration the convictions of others. I'm so thankful that I am free in you, and I am also grateful for the opportunity to focus on what truly matters in your kingdom.

Patient Growth

Now, those who are mature in their faith can easily be recognized,
for they don't live to please themselves but have learned to patiently
embrace others in their immaturity.

ROMANS 15:1

Mature faith does not overly focus on itself or its own convictions. Spiritual growth allows for the roots of our faith to grow deep into the soil of God's love, and with our roots firmly planted, we are not easily upset by those who don't see things the same way that we do. In our maturity, we are able to relate to those who are younger in their faith because we once were in their place.

Think of how loving parents direct their children. Do they despise their child's immaturity, or do they understand that there is much that the child cannot yet know because of their lack of life experience? Let us patiently embrace those in our faith circles who are young and learning, understanding that as they grow, they will grow in their perspective. Let's love one another deeply, recognizing that endurance and patience are fruits of the Spirit.

Jesus, thank you for your unending patience with us. Forgive me for where I have become disillusioned with those who have narrower views than I do. Give me grace-strength and patience and, most of all, love to live as an encourager.

March

Living Reflections

I will not be presumptuous to speak of anything except what Christ has accomplished through me. For many...are coming into faith's obedience by the power of the Spirit of God, which is displayed through mighty signs and amazing wonders, both in word and deed.

ROMANS 15:18–19

Paul had an illustrious ministry, traveling far and wide throughout the Roman Empire. Even so, he was not haughty and did not presume to be greater than anyone else. In his leadership, he established and encouraged many congregations of believers. He knew what it was to be well-known as a Jewish teacher, and he knew what it was to be humbled in his knowledge. Christ completely changed his perspective.

Paul knew that the only thing worth bragging about was the work that Christ had done. He knew the empowerment of the Spirit in his ministry, and he relied on the grace-strength of God to provide for him along the way. May we also rely on the mighty work of God in our lives more than we do our own accomplishments. Let us humble ourselves before the Lord and be living reflections of his mercy "both in word and deed."

Jesus, I want to reflect your power in my life. I don't want to be wise in my own eyes; I'd rather lean on your understanding and the power of your Spirit than my own.

Word of Caution

Watch out for those who cause divisions and offenses among you.
When they antagonize you by speaking of things that are contrary to
the teachings that you've received, don't be caught in their snare!

ROMANS 16:17

The Spirit of God brings unity. Those who seek to turn brothers and sisters against each other are not walking in the love of God. Where there is the insatiable urge to debate and antagonize, without regard for the other person's point of view, lies a trap. May we be wise in our dealings, and may we be discerning in whom we allow to influence our perspectives.

Where there is love, where there is unity, where there is peace, where there is forgiveness and reconciliation, there is the Spirit of God at work in his people. Let us throw off our offenses and stay away from those who are simply looking to argue their opinion. There is wonderful connection in a community that does not shrink back from hard topics but approaches them with compassion, understanding, and acceptance.

Lord, I want to walk in the wisdom of your Spirit, recognizing the fruit of your work. Where there is division, I will not add my brick to the wall of dissension. I want to partner with your perfect peace and love that breaks down walls of hostility.

Instruments of Goodness

I'm so happy when I think of you, because everyone knows the testimony of your deep commitment of faith. So I want you to become scholars of all that is good and beautiful, and stay pure and innocent when it comes to evil.

ROMANS 16:19

In his benediction to the Romans, Paul honors their faith. He encourages them to keep pursuing what is good and beautiful, staying pure and innocent in the Spirit and rejecting what is divisive and crude. May we find encouragement, too, in this proclamation.

We become instruments of God's goodness when we align with his kingdom values. When our lives are built on the love, peace, joy, justice, mercy, kindness, and power of God, they will reflect it in the fruit of our relationships. Let's stay the course, remaining deeply committed in our faith and leaning on the Spirit of God who brings unity to his people.

Holy Spirit, I want to be an instrument of your goodness. I want to know the power of your mercy in my life and walk in compassion. May my life be a reflection of your great grace as I walk in your ways.

More than Enough Power

I give all my praises and glory to the one who has more than enough power to make you strong and keep you steadfast through the promises found in my gospel; that is, the proclamation of Jesus, the Anointed One.

ROMANS 16:25

After Paul had shared his message with the Roman church, he gave all the praise and honor to God, whom he recognized as the only one who could make them strong and keep them steadfast.

Who of us has not been worried about a loved one? We can, and should, offer them wisdom when they are receptive. We should encourage them in God's love to live in the light of his goodness. And still, at the end of the day, it is only God's power, not our words, that can sustain and strengthen each person in their faith. Let's do what we know to do, but it is not our responsibility to carry the burden of their choices. Let's continue to support and encourage them, all the while giving God the praise and glory, for he will be their help.

Great God, only your power is strong enough to strengthen and sustain every heart that turns to you. I give you my worry about my loved ones, and I trust you to do what I never could. Only you are in control.

Set Apart

You have been made pure, set apart in the Anointed One, Jesus.
And God has invited you to be his devoted and holy people,
and not only you, but everyone everywhere who calls on the name
of our Lord Jesus Christ as their Lord, and ours also.

1 CORINTHIANS 1:2

We are part of a global body of believers and not only connected to the isolated churches that we attend. We have been set apart as God's own, a holy people! No matter our culture or language, when we are in Christ, we are unified with everyone who lives under the banner of his love.

May you find that your devotion goes beyond your understanding of who God is and how he relates to you. May you look for ways to extend love to others through service and generosity, no matter the differences you have. When compassion leads you, God is in it.

Lord, thank you for setting me apart as your own and for welcoming me into the diverse family of your kingdom. I am honored to be yours, and I know that there are people from every tribe, nation, and language that belong to you too.

Extravagant Wealth

In him you have been made extravagantly rich in every way.
You have been endowed with a wealth of inspired utterance
and the riches that come from your intimate knowledge of him.

1 CORINTHIANS 1:5

We find the kind of wealth that lasts in the Spirit. It is based not in the overabundance of money, privilege, or status, but in the kingdom of Christ. The Spirit's fellowship is abundantly accessible to all who come to Christ. There is a wealth of gifts to partake of in him! There are gifts of speaking, which includes prophecy, tongues and interpretation of tongues, preaching, and teaching the Word of God.

These are wonderful gifts! And yet the greatest gift is knowing God and being known by him. Everything else is extra. May you find your soul satisfied in the generosity of God's presence with you. Lean into his nearness and spend time fellowshipping with him in prayer and meditating on his Word. Taste and see that the Lord is good.

Loving Lord, I want to know greater satisfaction in your presence. Fill me with your revelation-knowledge and speak to my heart with your words of life. Revive my heart and satisfy my soul with your good gifts.

Held Fast

He will keep you steady and strong to the very end, making your character mature so that you will be found innocent on the day of our Lord Jesus Christ. God is forever faithful and can be trusted to do this in you.

1 CORINTHIANS 1:8–9

As we follow the Lord with willing and yielded hearts, he keeps us steady and strong. No matter the troubles we face or the trials that test us, he is with us to the very end. He is our very foundation, and his love will never let us go. His Spirit works in our hearts to refine us; our character is cultivated in his presence.

May the roots of your confidence go deep into the faithfulness of God. You can trust him with all that you are. You can trust him with your deepest desires and your most treasured gifts. He cares for you, and he cares about what concerns you. He will continue to hold you steady in his love. Lean back into his mercy and let go of the worry that keeps you from resting in him.

Jesus, I trust you more than I trust anyone else. Hold me steady when my world is shaking. I believe that you are forever faithful, and I can rely on you.

Message of Power

To preach the message of the cross seems like sheer nonsense to those who are on their way to destruction, but to us who are being saved, it is the mighty power of God released within us.

1 CORINTHIANS 1:18

What does it look like to proclaim the message of the cross in our lives? Does it only count when we are speaking in front of crowds, or does the testimony of his power move as strongly when shared one-on-one? Surely, we know that God can use our willingness and do with it far more than we ever could.

The wisdom of God is given to those who are teachable and humble. True wisdom is rooted and established in the mercy of God. May we live the message of humble reliance on God's power at work within our lives. May we be willing vessels, not only when others are watching but even much more when no one notices. Every proclamation of Christ counts. Every movement in compassion reflects his work in our lives.

Lord Jesus, thank you for the power of your love at work in the lives of those who look to you. I want my life to reflect your love in every detail.

No Need to Impress

My brothers and sisters, when I first came to proclaim to you the secrets of God, I refused to come as an expert, trying to impress you with my eloquent speech and lofty wisdom.

1 CORINTHIANS 2:1

You don't need a degree in biblical theology to live a life of true faith. You don't have to be in a formal ministry or have gone to church all your life to serve God. Psalm 19:7 states: "Yahweh's laws lead us to truth, and his ways change the simple into wise."

It is enough to follow the Lord with a surrendered heart, walking in the ways of his kingdom and not the wisdom of this earth. His revelation-truth is simple. His pathways of peace, mercy, and kindness are open to all who come to him. Let us throw off the things that complicate our faith and get back to the simple gospel. If Paul did not use his status to impress others, we should not either. Let us, with humble hearts and surrendered lives, live for the audience of the Lord. None of us is more worthy of God's love than any other.

Lord, I give up the need to impress others and live from a heart of authenticity and integrity. Your principles are the only ones that truly matter.

Holy Spirit Wonders

The message I preached and how I preached it was not an attempt to sway you with persuasive arguments but to prove to you the almighty power of God's Holy Spirit.

1 CORINTHIANS 2:4

P aul leaned on God's strength in his weakness and in doing so, understood the great power of God was much greater than anything he could offer on his best day. The Holy Spirit is the power of God at work in our lives. His living and active Spirit within us is the strength of our souls.

In 2 Corinthians 12:10, Paul goes on to say even more about relying on God's strength: "For when I feel my weakness and endure mistreatment…I am made yet stronger. For my weakness becomes a portal to God's power." May you look at every trial you face and every weakness you feel as an opportunity. It is an opportunity for the almighty power of God's Spirit to work in wonders. "For God intended that your faith not be established on man's wisdom but by trusting in his almighty power" (1 Corinthians 2:5).

Spirit, I welcome you to do with my weakness what only you can. Have your way in my life and work miracles of restoration, redemption, healing, and power.

Spirit to Spirit

After all, who can really see into a person's heart and know his hidden impulses except for that person's spirit? So it is with God. His thoughts and secrets are only fully understood by his Spirit, the Spirit of God.

1 CORINTHIANS 2:11

What hides in our hearts is only known to us and to God. He reads our hearts like an open book, and he understands more about us than we realize. He sees every intention and every hurt. He knows the motivations of our actions even more clearly than we do.

The Spirit of God knows the motivations of the Father's heart just as well. The Spirit imparts the truth of the Father's love to us. He ministers peace, joy, comfort, and strength. He is the lifter of our heads and the source of our hope. He goes beyond the outer layers of our lives to minister straight to our hearts, from deep unto deep, Spirit to spirit. What a wonderful reality this is!

Holy Spirit, minister to the depths of me, even now as I focus on you. Draw near and fill me with your loving presence. I long for the peace you bring and the clarity you offer. Thank you.

Spirit Wisdom

Those who live in the Spirit are able to carefully evaluate all things,
and they are subject to the scrutiny of no one but God.

1 CORINTHIANS 2:15

When we rely solely on our own human understanding, the revelation of God does not make sense to us. His kingdom is superior to our own, and his values supersede any of our earthly principles. God is pure and kind, not flexing his strength and power to intimidate. There's no need for him to shout to get our attention. He does not manipulate us or hide ulterior motives.

May we live in the wisdom of God, leaning on his Spirit to reveal his love in greater measure. Let's follow the values that Christ taught. His ways are better than our own. Though we may think that self-protection and pride can keep us safe, the most peaceful place to reside is in the yielded surrender of our heart to his.

God, you are my leader, and I live according to your values. I trust that your Spirit at work within me will continue to illuminate your ways more and more. Thank you for your discernment.

Coworkers in Christ

Now, the one who plants and the one who waters are equally important and on the same team, but each will be rewarded for his own work.

1 CORINTHIANS 3:8

Whether we view our gifts or roles through the lens of pride or of grounded humility, let us not give in to the idea that we are either more important or less important than another. Paul clearly says in this that whatever the role, we are *equally important*, working for the same team. Our lives are not a competition against one another; we are striving for the same thing—for Christ to be known and glorified.

God brings the supernatural growth, as Paul says in the preceding verse. It is his work to grow, and we are honored to partner with his purposes. May we look for every opportunity to encourage one another as we work for the shared goal of being living images of Christ's love in every area of our lives. We are coworkers under the leadership of our Lord Jesus Christ.

Jesus, I don't want to compete in pride or shrink in shame, falling into the trap of comparing myself with my brothers and sisters in you. I want to be a pursuer of peace and unity in your great, powerful love, pointing others to you.

God's Garden

We are coworkers with God
and you are God's cultivated garden,
the house he is building.

1 CORINTHIANS 3:9

There are no celebrities in the kingdom of heaven. Though we are prone to idolize people, putting them on pedestals and removing their humanity, we are all the same in Christ. He does not show favoritism, and his loyal love is extended in the same abundant measure to all. May we reflect his love by tearing down the walls of division that stand between us.

Each of us is a flower in the garden of our God. He is cultivating us in his kingdom, and he is building upon the foundation of our lives. Whatever growth we experience is under his hand. When we are trimmed back, he is pruning us so that our lives will experience even greater growth. May we stay grounded in the love of God, and may we be quick to trust his steady hand.

Good God, you are the master gardener, and whatever you put your hand to brings life, hope, and restoration. I trust you with my little life. I want to be like you—a unifier, not a divider, and a truth speaker, not an opinion spewer.

God's Standard

God has given me unique gifts as a skilled master builder who lays a good foundation. Afterward another craftsman comes and builds on it. So builders beware! Let every builder do his work carefully, according to God's standards.

1 CORINTHIANS 3:10

D o you use your unique gifts for the glory of God? Are you displaying his mercy through the work of your hands? It was Paul's unique gifts as preacher, teacher, and apostle that led him to travel widely and share the good news of Christ. We are all builders in our own way. What sphere do you find yourself in? Where have your gifts led you in life?

Use your craftsmanship with the integrity of the kingdom of God as your highest value. We are not all ministers and evangelists, and we don't have to be. Whatever you are gifted in, use it for the glory of God. How? By doing it well, with honesty, integrity, grit, and grace. Let all that you do be held up to God's standards, and you won't go wrong.

Lord, thank you for grace that empowers me to do right. When I mess up, grace will guide me into restoration. I keep my heart humble before you as I gladly partner with your purposes in my unique craft.

Fools for God

So why fool yourself and live under an illusion?
Make no mistake about it,
if anyone thinks he is wise by the world's standards,
he will be made wiser by being a fool for God!

1 CORINTHIANS 3:18

Deceit is not something that only happens from the outside in. We can also fool ourselves. When we think we know best in every area, we deceive our own hearts. When we remain humble and teachable, the wisdom of God will guard us and guide us, even through self-deception. Let's not let pride shut the ears of our hearts, for there is wisdom to guide, instruct, and liberate us in the presence of God.

What does it mean to be a "fool for God"? It means laying aside our allegiances to any human leader, letting Jesus be our true leader. It looks like living by the wisdom of Christ's kingdom and not by the status quo or the popular trends of the day. No one can fool God, so we know that we can trust him to guide us in the purity of his truth.

God, I recognize that I can convince myself of many things. I don't want to harden my heart against your voice or resist your wise leadership. I humbly surrender to you, God.

Important Qualities

The most important quality of one entrusted with such secrets is that they are faithful and trustworthy.

1 CORINTHIANS 4:2

Paul was speaking here of the apostles who helped establish the church, labeling them stewards of Christ and servants of God. They had been entrusted with God's mysteries as willing ones who set the church in order. Just as it was important for the apostles of Paul's day to be faithful and trustworthy, so it remains today for each of us who serve the Lord.

Are you a trustworthy friend, partner, and worker? Are you faithful to do what you promised to? It is not a requirement for every follower of God to be an apostle, a teacher, or a leader of a church. Even so, faithfulness and trustworthiness are qualities that will always be highly valued in God's kingdom. Make sure that they are true of those in leadership to whom you submit, for God's standards have not changed through the ages.

Great God, I want to be a person of my word, known for my love for others, faithfulness, and trustworthiness in every area of my life. Refine me and continue to transform me into your image as I do the work before me.

Wait Patiently

Resist the temptation to pronounce premature judgment...Instead, wait until the Lord makes his appearance, for he will bring all that is hidden in darkness to light and unveil every secret motive of everyone's heart. Then, when the whole truth is known, each will receive praise from God.

1 CORINTHIANS 4:5

Though we may be quick to judge, God is patient in mercy. It is not our job to judge what we do not know the inner workings of. This is not to say that there is not a place for accountability. We cannot right every wrong that we witness in this world, especially from the outside in, but we can continue to partner with the heart of God as we wait for him to return.

Jesus will one day bring every hidden thing to light, and he will reveal the motivations of each of our hearts. Instead of judging others for their differences of opinions, let's let love line our hearts. It's God's job to judge, and it is ours to follow his lead of mercy. He is so full of grace and compassion. Let's not take for granted his love, for it is our saving grace as much as it is anyone else's.

Jesus, your mercy gives me patience and clarity. I don't need to judge others when you see everything clearly.

Ready to Reconcile

When we are slandered incessantly, we always answer gently,
ready to reconcile. Even now, in the world's opinion,
we are nothing but filth and the lowest scum.

1 CORINTHIANS 4:13

Even in the face of persecution, slander, and misunderstanding, we can persist in love. Paul sets this example and calls us to rise up to it with him. Jesus did not defend himself against mockers, so we don't need to either. Instead of stooping to the level of those who tear us apart with their words, let's move with compassion, ready to reconcile.

Someone's scorn often has a reason behind it. When we get curious about someone's reaction to us without placing judgment on it, we are open to compassion. Perhaps those who criticize us relentlessly have felt the failure of living up to others' expectations in their own lives. Maybe the ones who ridicule are themselves full of shame. In any case, let's be ready with gentleness and willingness to forgive.

Jesus, when I let go of the need to control how others perceive me, I am free to just be me and to love without condition. Thank you for your mercy-kindness that leads me to life. May I be a living reflection of your kindness.

Loving Correction

> Although you could have countless babysitters in Christ
> telling you what you're doing wrong, you don't have many fathers
> who correct you in love.
>
> 1 CORINTHIANS 4:15

How would you rather be corrected—by being scolded, by pointing out the bar you're failing to reach, or by being lovingly corrected by someone who knows you well? Correction does not have to be shame-inducing. In fact, the correction of the Lord is always laced with kindness. He points out who we are, who he knows us to be, and lovingly calls us up to that.

Just as Christ corrects us in kindness, so should we seek to do the same with those we are in leadership over. Whether they are our children or our employees, someone we know will need correction at times. Do we choose to lead in love, calling them up to their true identities, or do we diminish them to failed actions? Let us be like Paul was, a loving parent to correct them.

Jesus, I am so thankful for your kind correction in my life. Whenever I have to give feedback, may I choose kindness as the lead, and clearly communicate their value and what needs to be changed. Thank you for your help.

Close in Spirit

Even though I am physically far away from you,
my spirit is present with you.

1 CORINTHIANS 5:3

It is possible to be far away from those we care about and to still be close in spirit. Love closes the miles between us. Today is a good day to reach out to those we love and to tell them just how connected we remain in our hearts to them.

Have you ever received a text, letter, or call from someone who is dear to you telling you that they were thinking of you? How did it make you feel? Love is not bound by time and space; it is not reserved for those who are within our reach. Love lives in the spirit realm, binding heart to heart and keeping us connected even when we are physically distant. Anyone who has experienced a deep loss in life knows that love does not fade with death. It transcends this life! May we be people who share our love loudly and consistently as long as it is called today.

Spirit, thank you for your love that goes beyond my understanding. Thank you for the connection of love and that I get to give it freely. Thank you for beautiful fellowship with dearly loved friends and family.

Purified and Holy

Some of you once lived in those lifestyles, but now you have been purified from sin, made holy, and given a perfect standing before God— all because of the power of the name of the Lord Jesus, the Messiah, and through our union with the Spirit of our God.

1 CORINTHIANS 6:11

No matter what our old lives looked like, when we are in Christ, we are new creations. He has purified us from all sin, and he has made us holy. We have been given perfect standing before God, not because of anything we have done or could offer but because of the mercy-kindness of Jesus Christ. He is our Savior and our covering.

The power of the name of the Lord Jesus is as strong today as it was when the Scriptures were written. The resurrection power of Christ is still working in our world and in our lives through his Spirit. We don't lack any good thing, for he is our strength and supply. He is the source of every good gift. What greater gift is there than our liberty in his love?

Jesus, you are my covering! You are my holiness and my right standing. I am covered in the perfection of your mercy. I press into you even more today, longing for deeper revelation, fellowship, and transformation.

Doing Good

It's true that our freedom allows us to do anything, but that doesn't mean that everything we do is good for us. I'm free to do as I choose, but I choose to never be enslaved to anything.

1 CORINTHIANS 6:12

P aul does not deny that our freedom in Christ is without limits. There are no ifs, ands, or buts to our liberty. And yet, we still have a higher calling in the kingdom of God to pursue loving-kindness, not only for ourselves, but also for those around us.

Whatever you do with your freedom, may you echo Paul's conviction to "choose to never be enslaved to anything." You are free to choose, and there is wisdom for you to choose what is good and beneficial if you will take it. You know your heart, what is driven by fear, shame, and pride, and what is driven by humility, love, and peace. Follow the fruit of the Spirit, and you won't go wrong.

Merciful God, thank you for the liberty I have to choose how to live. I'm not afraid to make mistakes, for your grace covers and meets me whenever I need it. I look to you as my loving leader, and I trust you to guide me into your goodness as I submit to your Spirit.

Mingling with the Spirit

The one who joins himself to the Lord
is mingled into one spirit with him.

1 CORINTHIANS 6:17

When we give our lives to the Lord, we join ourselves to him. We are made one in his Spirit, united in his mercy. In Romans 8:9, Paul says, "When the Spirit of Christ empowers your life, you are not dominated by the flesh but by the Spirit." His Spirit dwells within us, and we become his home.

Our bodies are the sacred temple of the Spirit, as Paul goes on to say in 1 Corinthians 6:19. "You don't belong to yourself any longer, for…the Holy Spirit, lives inside your sanctuary." As vessels of God's Spirit, our spirits mingle with his, and we are transformed by his life within us. What a beautiful and mysterious truth! May we expand in our understanding, our experience of his love in our lives, and in the power of his work within us.

Holy Spirit, I am your home, and I surrender to your leadership deep within. Lead my soul as I continually submit to you. Move in power, transforming my thoughts, my attitudes, and my heart in the values and wisdom of your kingdom.

Purchased by God

You were God's expensive purchase, paid for with tears of blood,
so by all means, then, use your body to bring glory to God!

1 CORINTHIANS 6:20

Our very lives were paid for with the precious blood of Christ. Our salvation is in him alone. Because we are God's expensive purchase, let's live to bring glory to God, the Savior of our souls! He is worthy of our whole lives, our whole surrender. He is trustworthy and full of mercy power to bring life out of the ashes of our defeat.

Goodness is coming—greater than anything we've ever known before. In the kingdom of our God, more love, more joy, more peace, more justice, more passion is in store. He has endless stores of his kingdom fruit. He is not finished moving in restoration power, so don't give up hope. Persevere in hope, leaning into his presence with you. Continue to live for him, and you will bring him glory.

Jesus, thank you for your sacrifice. I can't begin to rightly express my gratitude for your liberating love that sets me free. I live for you, Lord, for you are perfect, holy, and easy to please.

True Identity

Your identity before God has nothing to do
with circumcision or uncircumcision.
What really matters is following God's commandments.

1 CORINTHIANS 7:19

P aul often spoke of the breaking down of the divide between Jews and gentiles, exposing the heart of God as revealed through Jesus. Our true identity is not in our ethnicity, nationality, or any alignments we make in this world. It is found in our adoption as children of God.

The Jews knew circumcision to be the outward sign of God's covenant with Abraham and his descendants. Paul's statement that their identity had nothing to do with this was earthshaking. Instead of focusing on the outer things, Paul emphasized that inward transformation is what truly pleases God. This remains true today. No matter how you identify as a world citizen, what really matters is the inner submission and transformation of your heart in God's Spirit.

Lord, I lay down the pride I feel in my identity in this world, and I proclaim that my identity in you is all that truly matters. I see that I am no better than anyone else. Let the power of your mercy continue to transform me and my perspective of others.

Look for Opportunities

Everyone should continue to live faithful in the situation of life
in which they were called to follow Jesus.

1 CORINTHIANS 7:20

We do not have to change everything about our lives—
where we live, our jobs, our communities—in order
to follow Jesus. He will make it clear, as we follow him, what we
need to leave behind and what we need to integrate into our lives.
Though we could follow him to the ends of the earth, we don't
have to. He meets us where we are, transforming our current lives
with his incomparable power.

When was the last time you looked for opportunities to serve
God where you are instead of wishing for different circumstances?
His mercy meets you in your present moment. Even here, now, in
the spaces where you take up room, God is with you. Let your eyes
look for opportunities to serve him throughout your day. He is
faithful to lead, to transform, and to liberate you. Rely on his help.

*Good Shepherd, I often get distracted by what could be instead of
embracing what is true right now. Meet me in the messiness of my
mundane life and give me inspiration as I look for ways to honor
you in my life right now.*

Stay Close

Brothers and sisters, we must remain in close communion with God, no matter what our situation was when we were first called to follow Jesus.

1 CORINTHIANS 7:24

The most important thing we can do in this life is to remain in close communion with God. No matter what season we are in, no matter the trials or the celebrations we are experiencing, we can cultivate close relationship with God through the fellowship of his Spirit. He is near, willing to intervene where we need help, and full of kindness.

We are not slaves of God; we are beloved children. That means we have open access to the Father at all times. We don't need to hide anything from him. He knows us through and through, and he loves us relentlessly. May we discover, or remember, the joy of unending communion with our Maker. He accepts us as we are, washes over us with his pure mercy, and loves us to life again and again. He remains the same—yesterday, today, and forever!

Spirit of God, the aim of my life is to remain close to you. Thank you for uninterrupted communion with your Spirit. I love you. I am yours, and I long to know you more. Meet me here with your incomparable mercy.

Free from Anxiety

We are to live as those who live in the world but are not absorbed by it, for the world as we know it is quickly passing away. Because of this, we need to live as free from anxiety as possible.

1 CORINTHIANS 7:31–32

P aul was speaking of the urgency of the times that they were in, encouraging the readers to live in the world without taking on its skewed values. We live for an eternity that won't fade. We, too, are in times of urgency. Though fear may be a motivator in the world, it should not rule our decisions. Love is to be our guiding post. Mercy is to be our motivator.

We live in times that are constantly testing our trust. How can we live as free from anxiety as possible, as Paul encouraged? In some ways, this is a personal decision. What breeds anxiety and worry within you? Can you put boundaries around your time, attention, and information intake to combat this? Let the peace of God rule in your heart, trusting in his faithfulness.

Great God, I trust you more than I do any person. I trust that your power is at work even in the harshest climates. You are my hope, and I make more room to focus on you and less on the troubles that I can't control.

Love Leads to Understanding

> If anyone thinks of himself as a know-it-all,
>   he still has a lot to learn.
> But if a person passionately loves God,
>   he will possess the knowledge of God.

1 CORINTHIANS 8:2–3

When we promote our opinions as fact, especially in areas where there is clear liberty in God's kingdom to choose for ourselves, we lose sight of what truly matters. Pride is a shaky place to take a stand. When we build our lives on God's love, this love builds up not only us but also those around us. It will last forever, not cracking or shifting.

Paul was addressing the issue of food offered in sacrifice to idols (v. 1) here. He recognized that everyone seemed to have their own opinions and seemed to believe that they were right and others were wrong. Can you think of an issue in our world that echoes this? Have you participated in it? Instead of being puffed up over our opinions, may we let love be the foundation of every interaction and conversation. Let's passionately love God instead of our own opinions, for we will know God more as we do.

Loving Father, I don't want to misuse my freedom to excuse my pride. I don't want to be a know-it-all. I'd rather be a lover of you and others.

Source of Everything

Yet for us there is only one God—the Father. Out of him is all things,
and our lives are lived for him. And there is one Lord, Jesus,
the Anointed One, through whom we and all things exist.

1 CORINTHIANS 8:6

God is the ultimate source of every living thing. He is the
Creator, Maker, and Redeemer. All that we have is from
his hand, and all that we long for finds its origin in him. Instead
of chasing down our desires in the world and its empty promises,
let's look to the one who set the stars in motion and put the planets in their place.

The same God who breathed life into Adam and Eve, who
separated the darkness from the light, and who spoke the world
into existence, is the God who fathers us. Let's live for him, unashamedly and unabashedly. There is more goodness in him than
there is outside of him. There is more to discover in his kingdom
than any human has yet experienced. Let's not stop pursuing him,
for he is easily found and even more easily pleased.

*Creator, I believe that all I am looking for finds its truest form in
you. You are the perfect parent, partner, and friend. You are the
purest love I will ever know. You are the power I need to persevere,
and you are full of love. Thank you!*

April

Absolutely Free

Am I not completely free and unrestrained? Absolutely!
Am I not an apostle? Of course! Haven't I had a personal
encounter with our Jesus face-to-face—and continue to see him?
Emphatically yes!

1 CORINTHIANS 9:1

Just as Paul declared his own freedom in Christ, so we, too, can live in the liberty of God's love in our lives! Paul continued to have Christ in his sight, fixing his eyes on him throughout his ministry. Where are the eyes of our heart fixed? Where is our attention focused?

Even here, Paul is not simply speaking about his own freedom but also how the choices he makes affect others. In the last verse of the preceding chapter, Paul says that even though he could eat anything according to his own conscience, if it offended and hindered someone else's walk of faith, he would not eat it again. Do we also weigh our own liberty with the ways in which it affects those around us?

Lord, I know that I am completely free in you! Even so, give me a heart of love that considers how to live that freedom out without causing those I interact with to stumble.

Directed by the Lord

In the same way, the Lord has directed those who proclaim the gospel to receive their living by the gospel. As for me, I've preferred to never use any of these rights for myself.

1 CORINTHIANS 9:14

However the Lord directs us in life, let us honor his calling over us and over others. God is a good provider, and he will not let us waste away. Paul did not use his position of power to ask for support. He didn't want anything to stand in the way of the purity of his message. Though it is right for us to look for ways to support each other in love, manipulation has no part in the kingdom of Christ.

Paul was driven by the calling of God over his life to serve the church. Has God called you to step out in faith and follow him? Follow the direction of his leading and trust him to provide for you along the way. Use the skills you have and know that not every job you take along the way needs to be your passionate purpose. Paul was a tent maker at one point to fund his ministry. Know that you can be creative in your endeavors even as you trust God to provide.

Faithful Father, thank you for your provision and for your calling. I follow you, even in the day-to-day. I trust that you will partner with me even as I partner with you.

Gracious Living

> So then, where is my reward? It is found in continually depositing
> the good news into people's hearts, without obligation, free of charge,
> and not insisting on my rights to be financially supported.
>
> 1 CORINTHIANS 9:18

Paul did not need to be paid by those he ministered to in order to be effective in his ministry. An artist does not need to sell paintings in order to be an artist. A musician does not need to have paid gigs in order to be a genuine musician. So, a minister of the gospel is not verified once he is paid to do so.

How can you graciously live, fulfilling the gifts and passions of your heart as your reward? You do not need a paycheck to be who you were called to be. You don't need a contract to be justified in your path. We can work jobs that don't satisfy our passions and still pursue those passions without needing to be paid. Fulfillment isn't in the paycheck but in the act of doing what we love.

Lord, thank you for the reminder that I can live into my passions without needing to be compensated for them. You are my ultimate reward, and I know that you are better than any contract I could sign in this life.

Joyful Servanthood

Now, even though I am free from obligations to others, I joyfully make myself a servant to all in order to win as many converts as possible.

1 CORINTHIANS 9:19

Even though Paul was not obligated to others, he chose to joyfully serve all he could in order to show them the liberating love of Christ. He continued to deposit the good news of Christ into peoples' hearts without requiring anything in return.

How can we choose to joyfully serve others in our own lives? What areas are we drawn to and yet somehow resist because they seem insignificant or less worthy of our time? When our reward is in Christ, we don't have to limit our time to paying ventures. Though we cannot escape hard work or the responsibilities of family and friends, we can be creative in how we serve others in love. Let's partner with God's heart as we joyfully look for ways to reflect his love in our lives.

Jesus, you know the highs and lows of my life. You know what I enjoy and what feels insignificant. I joyfully partner with you in everything I do today—from the enjoyable things to the mundane. Be glorified in me.

Benefits of Adaptability

I became "weak" to the weak to win the weak. I have adapted to the culture of every place I've gone so that I could more easily win people to Christ. I've done all this so that I would become God's partner for the sake of the gospel.

1 CORINTHIANS 9:22–23

P aul was able to culturally adapt wherever he ministered. This did not mean that his core values changed from place to place, but he knew how to be sensitive to the cultures that he entered. He learned what was offensive to them and avoided doing those things. He participated with them in important aspects of their culture.

Flexibility and adaptability come more easily to some of us, but it is something that each of us can grow in. Our cultures largely mold and condition our thought patterns and inform our daily interactions. Are we aware of how our own culture has shaped us? Let's look for ways to be adaptable around those who are different from us, letting mercy lead us outside of our comfort zones.

God, I want to partner with your heart and your gospel, no matter who I'm around or what I am doing. Make my heart more sensitive to your leading and show me ways that I can share your good news with those who are different than I am.

Keep Running

Isn't it obvious that all runners on the racetrack keep on running to win, but only one receives the victor's prize? Yet each one of you must run the race to be victorious.

1 CORINTHIANS 9:24

Paul lived a disciplined lifestyle, training in perseverance and clinging to Christ in his calling. He was not perfect, as none of us are. He did, however, fix his eyes on the prize set before him. He aligned his life, every movement of it, in Christ. He depended on Christ more than he did his history as a leader and teacher of the law of Moses.

Whatever it is that is before you today, keep running your race. If you are tired, find your rest in him. If you are confused, drink from the living waters of Christ's presence, and let your vision clear in his wise coaching. Listen for his voice, follow his leading, and keep doing what is yours to do. Only you can keep running your race—no one else can do it for you. Keep trusting the Lord; he is faithful, and he will always be.

Jesus, fill me with your grace that empowers me to keep going when I feel like giving up hope. I trust your guidance more than I trust anything else. I am running to you.

Pictures of Perseverance

All the tests they endured on their way through the wilderness are a symbolic picture, an example that provides us with a warning so that we can learn through what they experienced.

1 CORINTHIANS 10:11

The Old Testament is full of examples of God's people wandering from him and coming back to him in repentance. God did not abandon them, even in their rebellion, but he restored them time and again with his mercy. Do we heed the lessons that history provides? Or do we think that we are unique, far-removed from the struggles that our ancestors faced?

Paul warned the readers of his letter in the following verse to "beware if you think it could never happen to you, lest your pride becomes your downfall" (v. 12). Humility is a hallmark of following Christ because we must face the limits of our humanity over and over again. Christ is our perfection. He is our salvation. Let's persevere in his love, repenting when we need to and letting his mercy-kindness cover our failures.

Lord, the longer I live, the more I see the need for perseverance. Help me to endure the hardships I face with grit and grace and meet me with mercy as I admit my own failures along the way.

Opportunities for Trust

We all experience times of testing, which is normal for every human being. But God will be faithful to you...each test is an opportunity to trust him more, for along with every trial God has provided for you a way of escape that will bring you out of it victoriously.

1 CORINTHIANS 10:13

Every trial is an opportunity to lean into the Lord. Will we let the troubles we face drive us from our peace in Christ, or will we press into his faithfulness with trusting hearts? It is normal for us to go through times of testing. Every person on this earth experiences hardship.

What we do in response is where our character is refined. Let's be people who trust that the Lord will be faithful to his Word. This does not mean that things will go as we expect them to; his ways are higher than our ways. Will we trust the loving-kindness of God and that he will show us how to stand up under our trials? He can bring us out of each one, victorious in him.

Faithful One, I trust that where I cannot see a way out of the trouble I'm in, you are leading me through with the steadfast hand of your righteousness. Fill me with your peace as I stand on your faithfulness.

Choosing Better

You say, "Under grace there are no rules and we're free to do anything we please." Not exactly. Because not everything promotes growth in others. Your slogan, "We're allowed to do anything we choose," may be true—but not everything causes the spiritual advancement of others.

1 CORINTHIANS 10:23

In our freedom in Christ, it is possible to choose a better way. Do our choices benefit the spiritual growth of others? Sometimes we need to make choices that are for the health and healing of our own souls. Even so, in Christ, we are all connected. We are a body of believers—a family of God.

Maturity does not simply look at freedom as a free-for-all. It recognizes that our choices have a ripple effect on those around us. There is tremendous liberty—greater liberty than we realize—in the love of Christ. When his mercy is our motivation, we choose better than what simply suits us. As we mature in the Lord, our choices take into account much more than our own preferences but also the spiritual health and growth of others.

Jesus, thank you for the incomparable liberty I have found in your love. As I grow in knowledge and relationship with you, I recognize how my choices affect those around me. Lead me into deeper purpose and peace as I choose your better ways.

Think of Others

Don't always seek what is best for you
at the expense of another.

1 CORINTHIANS 10:24

Paul repeats this theme throughout this chapter. Living for God's glory means taking into account how our lives intermingle with the lives of others. It means letting his love be our motivation and our barometer. His love is not just a personal experience—it is universal. It connects all living things. His love is immeasurable, and it takes others into consideration.

When we know that our convictions are in direct conflict with the convictions of others, we do not need to change them, but we should be able to adjust our choices in light of the offense they might bring. In verse 29, Paul says, "What good is there in doing what you please if it's condemned by someone else?" Liberty is ours, and yet there are still consequences to our choices, even when our own consciences are clear.

Lord, I'm so grateful that I don't have to be perfect to be right with you. I do want to honor others with my choices and not just myself. Help me to be loving and choose to forego offending others whenever possible.

Living to Honor God

Whether you eat or drink,
live your life in a way that glorifies and honors God.

1 CORINTHIANS 10:31

When we live to glorify God, we choose to submit to his leadership, his wisdom, and his love in our lives. We will never get it right all the time, so let's just take perfectionism off the table. That stunts our growth rather than promoting it. Our lives reflect the fruit of our hearts, and when we submit our hearts to Christ's leadership, the fruit of his Spirit will be evident.

As humans, we want to know the rules to follow, the ways we can fit the mold, and how we can be successful. Success in faith is not having it all together or being the loudest in the room. It is not how holy we appear to others. It is in the submission of our hearts to Christ, for he alone is our saving grace. He is our reconciliation. He is our final word. Let's live to honor him with hearts that are transformed in his living love.

Jesus, my highest aim is to honor you with my life. I want wisdom and discernment to be my teachers. I choose your ways over my own, and I live into your love.

A Good Example

Follow my example, for I try to please everyone in all things, rather than putting my liberty first. I sincerely attempt to do anything I can so that others may be saved.

1 CORINTHIANS 10:33

Paul was not being prideful when he instructed the church at Corinth to follow his example. In the matter of being adaptable and recognizing where others were in their faith journeys, he was able to adjust his own choices accordingly. Paul was not saying that they should all become itinerant missionaries. He was instructing them to put others' views and needs above their own preferences for the sake of the gospel.

How do you live your life? What are your top priorities, and are you able to adapt when faced with challenges? Are you an active part of your community? We were created for interdependence, and in relationship with others, we will have to put our own preferences on hold sometimes. Let's follow the example of Paul by not putting our own liberty first but by looking to connect with others in truth and in love.

Lord, I don't want to live with my own ideas as my driving force. Your love expands my understanding; it doesn't diminish it. May I reflect your mercy in my choices and in my interactions with others.

Under Christ

I want you to understand that Christ is the head of every person, and Adam was the head of Eve, and God is the head of the Messiah.

1 CORINTHIANS 11:3

C hrist is the source of every person. He is our High Priest, head over all creation. He is responsible for us, and we are covered under his covenant. Wherever we find ourselves today, may we know the peace, confidence, and belonging that comes with being yielded to Christ.

Whether man or woman, child or elder, we have no greater authority than Christ. He is the leader of our lives, the Savior of the world, and the liberator of all those who call upon him. We are one in him, even as a body is one. Though we do not look the same or perform the same tasks or purposes, we are unified in Christ as a living, breathing representation of his image on the earth. We each do our part, and we reflect a unique attribute of God.

Christ Jesus, you are the head of my life and the head of your church. Give me a clearer perspective of my small part in your kingdom and unify my heart with others in your love.

Equal before God

I have to insist that in the Lord,
neither is woman inferior to man
nor is man inferior to woman.

1 CORINTHIANS 11:11

In our faith traditions, as in the greater cultures of our modern-day society, we find that this is not a popular thought or opinion. Though Paul says here that man and woman are equal before God, neither one being either more favored or inferior, we find arguments to the contrary almost everywhere we look.

Both man and woman were created by God, and each has different roles and personalities. In the kingdom of Christ, men are not preferred. That is to say, in the kingdom of Christ, all are equally valued, equally loved, and equally worthy. The love of God does not prefer any one over another. It is abundant and overflowing; it is limitless, and it reaches us each in the same measure.

God, thank you for the equality we find in you. Even though there is inequality in this world, I know that it is not a reflection of you or your heart. I believe that we are all valued, all loved, and all offered the same liberation in your perfect mercy.

Testimony of Communion

Whenever you eat this bread and drink this cup,
you are retelling the story,
proclaiming our Lord's death until he comes.

1 CORINTHIANS 11:26

Communion is a practice that retells the story of Christ's sacrifice. Every time that we eat the bread, which signifies his body, and drink the cup, which represents the new covenant offered with his blood, we remember him. As we remember him, we proclaim the wonderful news of his redemption, both to our own hearts and to those who have yet to hear.

Take some time today, whether with others or on your own, to take the sacrament of communion. As you eat the bread, remember his body that was broken for you. As you drink the cup, remember that his blood was spilled for you. In his blood, you have been set free! There is glorious redemption in the resurrection power of his Spirit life within you. Remember, and as you do, testify to his goodness.

Jesus, thank you for sacrificing your body to break down the barriers that stood between the Father and us. As I take communion today, move within my spirit. I honor you.

Search Your Heart

So let each individual first evaluate his own attitude
and only then eat the bread and drink the cup.

1 CORINTHIANS 11:28

When we take communion, as we do anything in this life, it is our responsibility to evaluate our heart attitude. Let us humble ourselves, remembering how much, in our humanity, we rely on the Lord and his power to save. It is his work in us that redeems, restores, and sets us free.

Have you experienced the transformative power of God's love in your life? Have you known the humbling of your own ideas, opinions, and experiences in light of the power of God's mercy? Take time to search your heart and invite the Spirit to highlight areas that are out of line with his truth. Ask him to bring revelation of his higher perspective and respond to his leading.

Lord, I take time to search my heart today, along with the help of your Spirit. Move in me, refine my thoughts, and reveal areas that need a fresh touch of your mercy. I trust you to draw me with truth and the power of your love.

Same Spirit

The Lord Yahweh is one,
and he is the one who apportions to believers
different varieties of ministries.

1 CORINTHIANS 12:5

God is one—Father, Spirit, and Son. Different representations of the same being, God is unified and wholly connected. The three persons of the Trinity do not go against each other. In Christ, we are part of one body of believers. Though we have different roles, different expressions, and different gifts, we are connected in the Spirit. We serve the same Christ that our brothers and sisters serve.

May we not fall into the trap of idolizing certain gifts over others. The many gifts of the Spirit all have the same value. They each serve to glorify God in different ways but in the same measure. Instead of wishing we were differently abled, may we embrace the gifts that are already ours in the Spirit, while serving one another in love.

Holy Spirit, I recognize that you are one with the Father and the Son. I believe that what you have offered me is as good as what you offer others who submit to you. I honor your gifts in me, and may I use them for your glory.

A Variety of Miracles

The same God distributes different kinds of miracles that accomplish different results through each believer's gift and ministry as he energizes and activates them.

1 CORINTHIANS 12:6

God works in wonder-working power not only around us but also through us. He works different kinds of miracles through each of our lives. He activates the gifts he has given us through his Spirit, and he miraculously energizes our efforts with the movement of his power through our words and actions.

God is great, and he is greatly to be praised. His marvelous mercy is evident through how he meets us in power. His Holy Spirit is not only our comfort, our wisdom, and our strength, it is the very power of God to move in wonderful, awe-inspiring ways. Let's continually praise the Lord as he does his glorious work within us and through us.

Holy Spirit, thank you for your incomparable goodness at work within my life. I am yielded to your love, and I am your willing vessel. Continue to work your miracles in and through me.

Continuous Revelation

Each believer is given continuous revelation by the Holy Spirit
to benefit not just himself but all.

1 CORINTHIANS 12:7

The Holy Spirit chooses the gifts we receive from God. They are for the benefit of everyone and not just to build us up. The gifts of God reveal the fruit of his Spirit, they confirm the Word of God, and they also expand the kingdom of God in the earth.

There is continuous revelation into the ways of God through the Holy Spirit. There is an open invitation, an ever-flowing fountain of wisdom, that is available to those who are found in Christ. If there are areas of your life that are cloudy, look to the Spirit, who shines as bright as the sun, for wisdom and revelation. He will give you the discernment you need.

God of wisdom and revelation, I am so grateful for the sharp truth of your love. I am thankful to be part of your family. Continue to reveal to me the wonders of your kingdom. I am yours.

Spirit Work

> Remember, it is the same Holy Spirit who distributes, activates, and operates these different gifts as he chooses for each believer.
>
> 1 CORINTHIANS 12:11

Who are we to judge what God offers each of us? Isaiah 64:8 says, "We are the clay and you are our Potter. Each one of us is the creative, artistic work of your hands." Each of us is a unique expression of God's handiwork. So, too, are the gifts he imparts to us. Let us be grateful for the beautiful ways in which God has imprinted himself in our lives. Even so, we can long for and ask for more.

The Spirit's work in our lives has no limit. We can be grateful for what he has done, is doing, and will continue to do. Jesus said in Luke 11:13, "If imperfect parents know how to lovingly take care of their children…how much more will the perfect heavenly Father give the Holy Spirit's fullness when his children ask him." Ask the Lord to meet you in greater ways and lean into the fullness of the Holy Spirit.

Great God, thank you for the gifts you have given me. I don't take them for granted, and I won't waste time comparing my gifts to those others have. Even so, I long for more of you. Exceed my expectations with your glorious fullness.

One in Christ

Just as the human body is one,
though it has many parts that together form one body,
so too is Christ.

1 CORINTHIANS 12:12

After Christ resurrected from the grave and encouraged his followers, he ascended to the throne of his Father. He is glorified and enthroned in heaven. As the body of Christ on the earth, we are co-enthroned with him. Paul says in Colossians 3:1, "Christ's resurrection is your resurrection too." And in verse 4, he continues, "As Christ himself is seen for who he really is, who you really are will also be revealed, for you are now one with him in his glory!"

This is not a lone venture for any of us. We belong to Christ, and we belong to each other. Just as a hand belongs to the body it inhabits, so are each of us connected in Christ. There is no insignificant part, and we cannot simply perform our role without affecting the other parts of the body. May we be united in loving submission to Christ and may we love and honor each other as well.

Christ Jesus, I recognize how dependent I am on you and others. Instead of tunnel vision to excel in my own part without thought of how interconnected we all are, I will move with compassion and empathy. Thank you!

Beauty of Diversity

*A diversity is required, for if the body consisted of one single part,
there wouldn't be a body at all!*

1 CORINTHIANS 12:19

How often do we look at our own lives and think that we're missing the mark? We are not carbon copies of each other, and sameness is not what the Holy Spirit develops in us. The kingdom of God is as diverse as this world and its different ecosystems. Why would we devalue ourselves by comparing our lives to others when we are each unique?

Paul says it this way, "If the whole body were just an eyeball, how could it hear sounds? And if the whole body were just an ear, how could it smell different fragrances?" (12:17). We each have a distinctive function in the body of Christ and in this world. Let's embrace our purpose and do what is ours to do in the glorious freedom of our acceptance in him.

Lord, help me understand and accept that other people in my life have a different function than I do. Give me grace and liberty to embrace what you have offered me so that I can freely live for you in my own unique way.

Puzzle Pieces

You are the body of the Anointed One,
and each of you is a unique and vital part of it.

1 CORINTHIANS 12:27

Think of your life as a puzzle piece, a unique part of the whole picture. No one else can take your place. God is faithful, and he will continue to be, whether we are full of faith or are faithless. It is our joy and honor to partner with him though he does not need our surrender in order to fulfill his promises on the earth. Even so, there will never be another you in all creation.

When we submit our lives to Christ, he takes our lives and weaves them like threads into a grand tapestry of his mercy. Though he does not need us, he delights in partnering with us. He loves to transform our lives in his living love. Let's choose the better way by leaning into his presence and following on the pathway of his mercy. He leads us into the abundance of his peace, love, joy, and hope as we cling to him.

Lord, thank you that I am an original and that you love me the way I am. I choose to submit my heart, my life, and my hope to you. You are better in every way than anything I find outside of you.

Pure Purpose

If I were to be so generous as to give away everything I owned to feed the poor, and to offer my body to be burned *as a martyr*, without the pure motive of love, I would gain nothing of value.

1 CORINTHIANS 13:3

The purest purpose we will ever have in life, the most fundamental motive of the kingdom of Christ, is found in love. Whatever we do, if it is with the pure motive of love in our hearts, it is a reflection of the mercy-heart of God.

We can gain nothing in making a name for ourselves in this earth. Though we may experience privileges within this life by our notoriety, we cannot take any of that with us when our bodies fail us. Whatever we do—whatever good we do, whatever we seek to serve and to gain with our lives—let it be with the purpose of being a living reflection of Christ's love in us.

Jesus, I want to live according to your love that does not simply show us with outer acts but with true belonging in you. I don't want to put conditions on my own love because I know you never do. May your love be my purpose and motivation.

Incredible Lengths

Love is large and incredibly patient.
Love is gentle and consistently kind to all.
It refuses to be jealous when blessing comes to someone else.
Love does not brag about one's achievements
nor inflate its own importance.

1 CORINTHIANS 13:4

Love does not pick and choose who gets to be its recipient. Love is an ever-flowing river, touching everything in its path. When Paul says that love is incredibly patient, this includes within difficult relationships. It does not leave openness to bitterness. It is consistent in kindness to all people.

None of us is perfect in love, but we are all perfected in the pure love of Christ. We are continually being transformed by its power. As our own lives are altered by mercy, we are able to choose love in our attitudes, in our relationships, and in our communities. We are fully covered in the abundance of God's affection without need for jealousy or inflating our own importance. Love grounds us.

Jesus, your love transforms me from the inside out. It gives me strength in my spirit, it gives me power to persevere, and it keeps me humble. Thank you.

Respect and Honor

Love does not traffic in shame and disrespect,
nor selfishly seek its own honor.
Love is not easily irritated or quick to take offense.

1 CORINTHIANS 13:5

The image of love is Jesus. When we replace the word *love* with the name of Jesus, we can see that living with this kind of value-driven mercy and compassion is not simply an ideal. *Jesus does not traffic in shame and disrespect.* With kindness, Jesus calls us up in love. May we do the same with each other.

Love does not seek its own honor. When we idolize people who lift their own names, abilities, and ideals above others, we are not lifting up someone who is walking in godliness. Jesus did not seek his own honor—why, then, should we? It takes humility to walk the path of Christ's love. *Jesus is not easily irritated or quick to take offense.* What a wonderful truth! May we be like him, with grace-filled hearts that extend willingness to understand rather than shut others down.

Jesus, I want my life to be filled with your love not just as an ideal but how I actually live it out. May you be honored in my life as I follow, submit, and redirect according to your ways.

Honest Truth

Love joyfully celebrates honesty
and finds no delight in what is wrong.

1 CORINTHIANS 13:6

There is something extremely beautiful about honesty. It breaks through the walls we put up to self-protect against disappointment. Not every truth is pleasant, but every honest word spoken in love with vulnerability and humility is better than a fake pleasantry that glosses over the reality of the situation.

May you experience the refreshing relief of being honest today. Even if it is just being honest with yourself and God, will you lean into the uncomfortable truths that you have been avoiding? None of sees the full picture, which means none of us has it completely right. Ask the Holy Spirit for God's higher perspective and invite him to reveal his truth over your life, your situations, and your heart attitudes.

Spirit, I know that you delight in the truth in what is right. I want to be one who joyfully celebrates honesty, even at times when it makes me uncomfortable. Show me the safe spaces where I can be vulnerable, for I know that community is important, but I also know not everyone is able to support me in a way that reflects your love. Thank you for your discernment.

Beyond the Known

Love never stops loving. It extends beyond the gift of prophecy,
which eventually fades away. It is more enduring than tongues,
which will one day fall silent. Love remains long after words
of knowledge are forgotten.

1 CORINTHIANS 13:8

Anyone who has ever grieved a deep loss of a loved one knows the profound truth that "love never stops loving." Though the person may be gone from our lives, no one and nothing can fill the void that they leave behind. Love is not limited, and therefore, it never needs to be replaced. Parents, too, know this well. When a family goes from one child to two (and beyond), our hearts expand in love. They are not diminished.

At the end of this life, even at the end of this world and all we have ever known, love will remain. May we give it the attention it deserves and let it lead us beyond what we've already known. Love will remain no matter where we go. Love will multiply as we meet more people and choose to open our hearts and lives, and it will never leave us.

Loving Lord, I have experienced the lasting power of love in my life, and I know that your love is even more pure, powerful, and steadfast. Continue to expand my understanding with deeper revelations of your incomparable mercy.

Just a Glimpse

For now we see but a faint reflection of riddles and mysteries as though reflected in a mirror, but one day we will see face-to-face. My understanding is incomplete now, but one day I will understand everything, just as everything about me has been fully understood.

1 CORINTHIANS 13:12

If Paul's understanding of Christ was limited, we must recognize our own limitations as well. Instead of letting pride puff us up, let's let humility guard our hearts and minds in Christ Jesus. Then we can stay teachable under the loving leadership of God, knowing that we all have equal access to the Father through Jesus.

Though we are limited in understanding the magnitude of God, one day we will stand face-to-face with the Almighty. Transforming love will bring us to this place. For now, let us be clothed in the loving-kindness of Christ, following in the ways he taught us to walk. He is with us through his Spirit, and there is more available in his fellowship than we can imagine. Let us keep going from glimpse to glimpse and glory to glory.

Jesus, though I know next to nothing, I have known the kindness of your presence, your love, your joy, your peace, and your hope in my life. I am so grateful to know you and to be known by you.

Eternal Source

Until then, there are three things that remain: faith, hope, and love—
yet love surpasses them all. So above all else, let love be the beautiful
prize for which you run.

1 CORINTHIANS 13:13

We cannot go wrong when aiming to live a life of liberating, loyal love. Faith and hope stem from love, making love the greatest virtue in the kingdom of God. Once we stand face-to-face with God, there will be no more need for faith and hope, for everything will be as clear as day before our very eyes. But love is eternal.

Love is loyal to the end. It lasts from generation to generation, and it reaches beyond us into the great unknown. No matter the twists and turns of our lives, the different locales or communities we have been a part of, the thread of God's mercy is a through-line. We have never been without his love, and we never will be. May we let it transform the ways we relate to others. Living love is our eternal source.

Jesus, thank you for the incomparable lengths of your love. No one can perceive the parameters of its power. Give me a greater glimpse of your mercy today in my own life.

May

Deeper Desire

I would be delighted if you all spoke in tongues, but I desire even more that you impart prophetic revelation to others. Greater gain comes through the one who prophesies than the one who speaks in tongues, unless there is interpretation so that it builds up the entire church.

1 CORINTHIANS 14:5

It is a wonderful thing to desire spiritual gifts. Paul says in verse 1 of this chapter that "it is good that you are enthusiastic and passionate" about these things. Every spiritual gift benefits the bearer of the gift, but all are not as beneficial to others. This is why Paul says that his own desire is that the church at Corinth be able to impart prophetic revelation to others.

Why prophetic revelation, you might ask? In verses 3 and 4, Paul answers this question: "When someone prophesies, he speaks to encourage people, to build them up, and to bring them comfort…the one who prophesies builds up the church." We should earnestly desire the gifts that help to build each other up.

Lord, thank you for the gifts that you give so freely to your children. I don't want to just receive and partake; I want to use what you give me to benefit those around me. Build me up so that I may also build others up.

Strengthened Focus

You are so passionate about embracing the manifestations of the Holy Spirit! Now become even more passionate about the things that strengthen the entire church.

1 CORINTHIANS 14:12

It is good to be passionate about the things of God and of his kingdom. It is wonderful when we are boiling over with affection and emotion toward the Lord and each other. Even so, Paul encourages that we become *even more passionate* about the things that strengthen the whole church.

Where is your focus in your spiritual life? What drives you? Where is your passion directed? Use these questions as a jumping off point to consider where you can grow in service, in love, and in connection with others. There is tremendous benefit in serving one another in love, promoting peace, and joyfully honoring the legacy of the Lord Jesus in our lives—in our homes, in our workplaces, and in our communities.

Lord, strengthen my focus in you. I don't want to be so focused on the wondrous mysteries of your kingdom that I forget to build up others in your love. The connection we have in fellowship with each other and you is what I want to be concerned with most of all.

Wise Thinking

Beloved ones, don't remain as immature children in your reasoning. As it relates to evil, be like newborns, but in your thinking be mature adults.

1 CORINTHIANS 14:20

The life of faith is not stagnant. We are constantly growing in faith, even as we mature in age. When we think of our spiritual growth in the same way that a person develops through their lifetime, we are able to see our different stages of faith as developmental.

When we are born again in Christ, we are like newborn babies. We do not go from infant to teenager overnight, so let's give each other grace in the stage we are in. We can be innocent to the evil of this world even as we grow. We can reason as mature adults while remaining pure in surrendered hearts to Christ. Wisdom's message is the same, no matter how old we are. Let's lean into the simple message of the gospel, for there we find freedom to live in Christ's love every step of the way.

Jesus, thank you for the reminder that we are all in different parts of our faith journey. I will not be disappointed or prideful if my spiritual maturity is different than someone else's. At the same time, I let wisdom be my great counselor.

Build Up

When you conduct your meetings, you should always let everything be done to build up the church family. Whether you share a song of praise, a teaching, a divine revelation, or a tongue and interpretation, let each one contribute what strengthens others.

1 CORINTHIANS 14:26

When our focus is on building each other up, encouragement will become second nature to us. What strengthens us will sometimes push us beyond our own experience and comfort. When we seek restoration from someone we have wronged, it is a strengthening act. When we vulnerably share a testimony of God's goodness with someone else, it can build up someone else's faith.

Strength training, as in spiritual building, is not a comfortable, easy thing. It stretches us, challenges us, and requires our willingness. Even so, it is beneficial. As we build each other up in the loving truth of Christ, we will find we are much stronger together than any of us is on our own. A family can carry more than a single person can. Let's not forget, then, the importance of faith-filled community.

Lord, thank you for calling me your own and placing me in your family. Though I've been accustomed to powering through on my own, I know that I can find true strength in the grace-empowered company of others and the loyal love of your people.

Firmly Fastened

It is through the revelation of the gospel that you are being saved,
if you fasten your life firmly to the message I've taught you,
unless you have believed in vain.

1 CORINTHIANS 15:2

The power of the gospel is in the message of the Messiah. Through his death and resurrection, we have our salvation. If we fasten our lives firmly to the message of Jesus Christ and his ministry, sacrifice, and resurrection from the dead, then we can know that our belief is not in vain.

Christ is King over all creation. He is worthy of our submission, worthy of our praise, and worthy of our trust. He is alive, seated at the right hand of his Father in heaven, and his Spirit is moving throughout the earth, within his church, and in our very hearts and lives. With Christ as our head, we follow his lead of mercy. We will find our joy in his fellowship, even in our sufferings. He is better than any other. What a wonderful Savior he is!

Lord Jesus, in your resurrection power, I come alive. I trust that you will continue to hold me close as I fasten my life to your truth. I cling to you.

Reality Check

Yes, I am the most insignificant of all the apostles,
unworthy even to be called an apostle,
because I hunted down believers
and persecuted God's church.

1 CORINTHIANS 15:9

Paul does not diminish his history of hostility against Christ's followers. He doesn't pretend that he has always followed the Lord. He is well aware of his life before his radical encounter with Jesus, and he reminds his readers of this. Humility goes a long way in relating to others and gaining their trust. Prideful boasts of our own accomplishments may impress some, but they will alienate others and perhaps alter our own self-perception.

When we lead with humility and vulnerability, admitting our faults and being honest about our shortcomings, we open the door for others to trust us in a deeper way. Paul admits that it is God's grace that has allowed him to minister, even multiplying his efforts. When we persevere in grace-strength, we are pushing through by the empowering presence of God with us.

Gracious One, you are my strength and my hope. You are the power of my testimony. I will not run from my story. I will share it with others and praise you for your empowering grace that has transformed my life.

Resurrection Life

The message we preach is Christ, who has been raised from the dead. So how could any of you possibly say there is no resurrection of the dead?

1 CORINTHIANS 15:12

The gospel has no message without Christ at its center. Christ *is* the message. His death was the ultimate expression of God's laid-down-love. The power that resurrected him from the grave three days later is the same power that lives in us through his Spirit today. His life has become our hope. We are covered in his compassion, and we are empowered by his transformative mercy.

What areas of your life are crying out for restoration? God is the Redeemer, and he has not stopped working in miraculously wonderful ways in the earth. As you wait on him, trust him. As you trust him, let your hope be set on his work. Even as Christ rose from the dead, so will we. When Jesus is the Lord of our lives, we have the promise of eternal life with him, no matter what we walk through now.

Messiah, your resurrection life is my hope. Revive my heart in your merciful truth and lighten the heavy load of worry I give to you. Thank you.

Victorious

We thank God for giving us the victory as conquerors
through our Lord Jesus, the Anointed One.

1 CORINTHIANS 15:57

No matter what you are facing today, you have everything
you need in the very real presence of the Spirit of God.
Christ's victory is your victory. His grace is your grace. His freedom is your freedom. Lay it all out before the Lord—every worry,
every need, and every thought.

However long it's been since you have felt the empowered
presence of God with you, know this: he is your present strength
and help. It doesn't matter how you feel or don't feel. You are victorious because you are in Christ. His living love covers you. Yield
your heart to him, give him your trust, and ask him to refocus
your perspective with his clarifying wisdom. Lean into his grace,
for it is close.

*Jesus, thank you for the victory that is mine in you. You have
conquered sin and death, and I am covered by your covenant. Settle
my heart in your peace and transform my heart as you speak your
living words of life over me today.*

Unshakable Foundation

So now, beloved ones, stand firm, stable, and enduring. Live your lives
with an unshakable confidence...we are assured that our union with the
Lord makes our labor productive with fruit that endures.

1 CORINTHIANS 15:58

I n Matthew 7:24, Jesus said, "Everyone who hears my teaching
and applies it to his life can be compared to a wise man who
built his house on an unshakable foundation." Paul echoes Jesus'
words by encouraging the readers to "stand firm, stable, and
enduring...with an unshakable confidence."

Jesus is our immovable foundation. When we build our lives
on the Rock of Ages, standing firm on his truth, the house of
our lives will not be moved when rains and winds come blowing through. Times of testing will come, but the foundation of
Christ's love will not crumble. His mercy will not be moved. What
a confidence we have in him! Let's live as those who are confident
in the power of Jesus and his resurrection. His fruit will blossom
from our lives as we do.

*Lord Jesus, thank you for the immovable strength of your love. I
build my life upon the truth that you are alive, your teachings are
my guide, and your living presence is the source of my strength,
wisdom, and hope. I stand on you.*

Courage to Continue

Remember to stay alert and hold firmly to all that you believe.
Be mighty and full of courage.

1 Corinthians 16:13

Paul's benediction to his readers applies to us as well. We must remember to stay alert and to hold firmly to all that we believe. It is easy enough to get caught up in business as usual and let down our guards to what we are feeding our minds and hearts. Wisdom does not fall asleep though. It is always alert and always available.

When we walk with wisdom, we must also remember to be courageous. At some point or other in our lives, we will have to call upon our courage; we cannot escape the troubles that come knocking on our doors. But God is faithful, and his grace-strength is available at all times. When we are alert, remembering where our trust and confidence lie, we can face whatever comes our way with courage.

Mighty One, your name is above every other, and your glory shines brighter than the sun. As I look to you over and over again, refresh my vision with the clarity of your wisdom and fill my heart with boldness to keep trusting you.

Loving Kindness

Let love and kindness be the motivation behind all that you do.

1 CORINTHIANS 16:14

What are the motivations behind your actions? Today is as good a day as any to take stock of the motives that drive your life. If you're not sure where to start, begin by taking inventory of where you are directing most of your time and attention. Consider what values are playing out in your relationships, your home, and your community.

When you have a baseline, you can adjust as needed. Where do love and kindness come in? Do they motivate any of your lifestyle choices? Praise God for those areas. Where are they lacking? Ask the Lord for wisdom, focus, and strategies to adjust to his mercy as you align your heart with his. Ask him to transform your heart as you invite his voice to direct you in areas where you may need to give up some things and add others. He is faithful to speak and to guide. Will you let his mercy redirect your own motives?

Christ Jesus, I want my life to be full of your Spirit fruit, and I know that takes intentionality, surrender, and obedience to your voice. Show me where your love can increase in my life so that I can move from a place of greater compassion.

Blessings of Peace

May undeserved favor and endless peace be yours continually
from our Father God and from our Lord Jesus, the Anointed One!

2 CORINTHIANS 1:2

Paul started every letter he wrote with greetings and blessings. In this particular letter, Paul blessed the readers, praying that they would experience the magnitude of God's favor and endless peace. As you read this today, you are included in that same prayer.

When was the last time you blessed someone with such a prayer? As you receive the favor and peace of God, you are filled to pass on the same benediction to others. In your comings and your goings, in your interactions throughout your day, may you greet people with kindness. May you be an arbiter of God's plentiful peace to those around you.

Father, thank you for the peace and favor of your presence. I recognize that this is a gift that you give to all. Your presence is the place I find satisfaction, rest, and peace. I will partner with your heart and extend your peace and kindness to those I meet today.

Comfort Leads to Compassion

He always comes alongside us to comfort us in every suffering so that we can come alongside those who are in any painful trial. We can bring them this same comfort that God has poured out upon us.

2 CORINTHIANS 1:4

R eceiving comfort fills the wells of our compassion. God tends to us with mercy that sustains us. His comfort does not leave us or let up. It is our nourishing grace. This grace strengthens us to meet others where they are.

As we are comforted by the Lord, we are able to extend comfort to others in their own pain. God is a compassionate Father who is kind to his children. He does not yell at us when we are down, but he meets us in the dust of our disappointment. He ministers to us when we are weak with sorrow. He lifts us up when we cannot stand for our grief. As we partner with him, we become those who can sit with others in their sorrow, ministering to them when they are weak and uplifting them when they cannot move on their own. What a glorious gift is the compassion of Christ!

God, I know true compassion because of the ministry of your Spirit's comfort in my distress. Thank you for the relief you bring. I want to lift other's loads the way you lift mine.

Strengthened to Endure

The comfort pouring into us empowers us to bring comfort to you.
And with this comfort upholding you, you can endure *victoriously*
the same suffering that we experience.

2 CORINTHIANS 1:6

P aul says that more trouble equals more comfort. No matter
what we face, there is comfort in the presence of the Lord to
meet us. More comfort to us means more comfort to others. It is
a chain reaction of compassion that strengthens us in our resolve
to be people of peace and relief, looking for ways to pass on the
goodness we receive.

We can be encouraged by those who have gone before us,
experienced trials of many kinds, and endured. We have the same
promise of empowered strength that comes through the Holy
Spirit with us. The Spirit is full of power to victoriously endure all
types of suffering. We cannot avoid times of testing, but we surely
can experience the empowering presence of God through it.

*Mighty God, rain over me with your liquid mercy, filling me up
with the strengthening grace of your presence. I need you more than
I need anything. As you meet me, I am empowered to help others.
Thank you.*

Pure Motives

We rejoice in saying with complete honesty and a clear conscience
that God has empowered us to conduct ourselves in a holy manner
and with no hidden agenda.

2 CORINTHIANS 1:12

In today's world, it is difficult to find a powerful leader who has
no hidden agenda. Politicians tend to pander to their audience.
Powerful businesspeople often look to raise their bottom line and
net worth. Jesus did not operate the way that the world around
him did and neither should we.

With God's grace as our source of strength and purity, we
have no need to boast about how many followers we incur or the
size of the movement we are a part of. Joy in ministry, as in life, is
found in the satisfaction of the Spirit. God is not impressed with
our bank accounts, our influence, or our accomplishments. He
delights in our surrendered hearts. He looks past the outer trap-
pings of success to the motives of our hearts. May we value what
he values and live with clear consciences before him.

*Loving Lord, I know that I can't impress you. Thank you for love
that meets me where I am, even in my weakness. Mold me in your
loving-kindness and transform my life as I live for you.*

True Fulfillment

All of God's promises find their "yes" of fulfillment in him.
And as his "yes" and our "amen" ascend to God, we bring him glory!

2 CORINTHIANS 1:20

Jesus is the yes and amen of God. He is the Son of God, the fulfillment of the promises of Yahweh. All our hopes are tied up in him. Thankfully, he is victorious over sin and the grave; nothing stands in his way. He has removed everything that stood between the Father and us, demolishing the wall of sin that stood in our way. There is not even the thinnest veil left between us and his Spirit. What a beautiful and glorious reality!

May you find encouragement to trust God more today with your hidden hopes, letting his Spirit be the seal over your heart. You are secure in God's love, authenticated as God's very own, genuinely found in his affection, and approved by him. In his righteousness, you are righteous. May you be filled with his powerfully present peace.

Holy Spirit, you are the seal over my heart. Revive my hope in you and move in miraculous mercy to transform my life in your power. I am yours.

Partners in Joy

Instead, we are your partners who are called to increase your joy.
And we know that you already stand firm because of your strong faith.

2 CORINTHIANS 1:24

As believers in Christ, we do not dictate what others believe.
Paul did not do this, and we need not act as micromanagers
of God's merciful truth. We are partners with one another in the
gospel. Paul said that the goal of the apostles was as partners called
to increase their joy. Do we look for ways to increase the joy of our
brothers and sisters in Christ?

This can look a myriad of ways, but none of it looks like
control. Look to the fruits of the Spirit that Paul mentions in
Galatians. It is by these that we know that the Spirit is working in
our lives: "joy that overflows, peace that subdues, patience that
endures, kindness in action…" (Galatians 5:22–23). These are just
a few of the fruits of his work within us. May we be people who
reflect gardens of his glorious fruit as we partner with others in
cultivating growth.

*Lord, I want my life to reflect your living love that encourages and
strengthens others in joy, peace, kindness, and faith. Have your way
as I submit to your work in my heart and life.*

Discernable Grace

God always makes his grace visible in Christ, who includes us as partners of his endless triumph. Through our yielded lives he spreads the fragrance of the knowledge of God everywhere we go.

2 CORINTHIANS 2:14

When we live our lives yielded to Christ, letting him lead us in his unlimited love, he spreads the fragrance of his kindness everywhere we go. There is no place where we are without his mercy. The knowledge of his glorious grace emanates through our submitted lives, for he is faithful to his word and faithful to his people.

We have nowhere further to look than Christ for the visible mercy of God. His life, his ministry, his death, and his resurrection reflect the mercy-heart of the Father. We are partners in this great grace, following our victor into his triumph. What a wonderful honor is ours!

Jesus, thank you for partnering with your people in revealing your great grace through our lives. My life is yielded to your leadership. I trust you more than any other. May my life be a fragrant offering to you.

Undiluted Message

> For unlike so many, we are not peddlers of God's Word who water down the message. We are those sent from God with pure motives, who speak in the sight of God from our union with Christ.
>
> 2 CORINTHIANS 2:17

Christ empowers those whom he calls. No matter how difficult our challenges are in ministry and in life, God enables us to overcome through his Holy Spirit. We are not sellers of the gospel. The gospel's power stands on its own, and its message needs no alteration. Those who serve to profit themselves while taking advantage of others with the message of the gospel are not walking in the pure motive of Christ's mercy.

Love does not deceive, and it does not serve the self at expense of others. The message of Christ is full, unadulterated kindness that is free for all who will receive it. May we never put stipulations on the gospel message where Christ has not. The message of Christ is powerful, and it is liberty for all who walk in it.

Lord Jesus, I know that the power of your life, death, and resurrection is greater than we could ever exaggerate. I only want to reflect your love in my life, more than I want to satisfy myself.

Empowered Living

We don't see ourselves as capable enough
to do anything in our own strength,
for our true competence flows
from God's empowering presence.

2 CORINTHIANS 3:5

No matter how ill-equipped you feel to face what is in front of you, take heart and take hope in the empowering presence of God. You don't have to rely on your own strength, talents, and abilities to move God's heart. When you have nothing left to offer, no ideas of your own left to rely on, lean on the grace of God.

The grace of God partners with you to empower you in whatever you do. It is good to use your skills for God. It is wonderful to pursue the passions he has put on your heart. You won't always have the answers to your problems, and you will run out of energy to tackle them. In those moments, God is your great competence. He is your help, and he is more than able to do immeasurably more than you can imagine.

Spirit of God, I'm so grateful for your presence that never lets up or lets me go. I never need to go it alone in this life, and for that I cannot begin to thank you. Meet me with the power of your presence and lead me on.

Renewed Focus

He alone makes us adequate ministers who are focused on an entirely new covenant. Our ministry is not based on the letter of the law but through the power of the Spirit. The letter of the law kills, but the Spirit pours out life.

2 CORINTHIANS 3:6

The new covenant that Jesus ushered in is a covenant that leads to life. The day of Pentecost is a wonderful example of this. On that day, the Spirit was poured out over the masses and three thousand people received new life. What a glorious testimony of God's goodness.

Where is your spiritual focus? Are you more concerned with abiding by the letter of the law, with its formulas for success that no one can perfectly achieve? Or are you focused on the gospel of grace that liberates you to live from a place of love, boldly encouraging those around you in faith and in courageous hope? Lean into the Spirit, who is your confidant, companion, and helper in every way. There is more than enough love to restore, renew, and revive your heart, vision, and hope in him.

Spirit, it is your power that revives my weary soul. Do what only you can do as I rely on your strength, your leadership, and your fellowship. I look to you.

Bright and Radiant

Yet how much more radiant is this new and glorious ministry
of the Spirit that shines from us!

2 CORINTHIANS 3:8

When Moses was met with the splendor of God on the mountain where he received the Ten Commandments, his face shined radiantly because of the glory he encountered there. This glory faded away, and Moses hid his face behind a veil so that the Israelites could not watch it as it left him. Paul describes here how this old order passed away with the ministry of Christ.

We are those who have received a greater glory that does not fade away with time. The Spirit's radiance does not fade from us, for we have his presence with us at all times. This is the wonderful news of the new covenant. With lives yielded to Christ, trusting in his sacrifice as the final word over our sin, we have been purified in his love. The ministry of the Spirit shines from us, for we are his vessels.

Spirit, shine your radiance through me. My heart is open to you, Lord. Lead me, teach me, and fill me with your peace. May my life be a shining beacon of your glory.

Clear Vision

The moment one turns to the Lord with an open heart, the veil is lifted and they see. Now, the "Lord" I'm referring to is the Holy Spirit, and wherever he is Lord, there is freedom.

2 CORINTHIANS 3:16–17

E veryone who turns to the Lord Yahweh with an open heart is embraced by his mercy. What prevented them from seeing the glorious truth of Christ is lifted, and they can see with clear eyes of faith. When we experience this transformation in our vision, there is a deep understanding of what we could not perceive before.

Are there areas of your life that are cloudy with the fog of confusion? Are you unsure of what you believe? Whatever your heart needs today, you can find it in the presence of God with you. The Holy Spirit is your liberator and your wise Counselor. Ask him for clarity where you have none and trust the peace of his Spirit that passes all understanding. He gives revelation to seeking hearts.

Holy Spirit, I have experienced freedom in you before, and I long for a fresh touch of your liberating life within me. Redirect my vision and bring clarity to my confusion. I trust you.

Reflections of Glory

We can all draw close to him with the veil removed from our faces. And with no veil we all become like mirrors who brightly reflect the glory of the Lord Jesus. We are being transfigured into his very image as we move from one brighter level of glory to another. And this glorious transfiguration comes from the Lord, who is the Spirit.

2 CORINTHIANS 3:18

As we gaze at the beauty of our glorious Lord Jesus through meditation, prayer, worship, and fellowship with his Spirit, we are transformed in his image. The more time and attention we give something, the more it reflects in our thinking and our lives. As we draw close to the Lord, we become mirrors of his glory. As we turn toward him, we reflect his life-giving light.

We move from glory to glory as we gaze upon the beauty of Christ. This is something we can do anytime, anywhere. It is not reserved for moments in chapels or cathedrals, in prayer meetings or Bible studies. Wherever you are, you have access to the abundance of his glory.

Lord Jesus, I turn my attention to you today. Transform my thoughts, my heart, and my attitude in your living love. There is no one else like you.

Mercy Covenant

Now, it's because of God's mercy that we have been
entrusted with the privilege of this new covenant ministry.
And we will not quit or faint with weariness.

2 CORINTHIANS 4:1

We have no further to look for God's mercy than in our own lives. If we have submitted our hearts to him in hope and trust that Christ alone is our Savior, his mercy is already working within us. We do not earn his affection. We cannot make him love us more, and we cannot convince him to love us any less. He loves because he loves—it's that simple.

We each have a ministry before us with which Christ has entrusted us. It does not need to look like working in or for a church. Everything we do with the motive of love toward God and others is significant. In our jobs, in our friendships, and in our spheres of influence, we can have a lasting impact if we will persevere in compassion, humility, and integrity.

Merciful Lord, thank you for the miracles of your mercy. Remind me where you have already left your imprint on my life, and give me revived vision to live your love out loud.

Beacons of Light

God, who said, "Let brilliant light shine out of darkness," is the one who has cascaded his light into us—the brilliant dawning light of the glorious knowledge of God as we gaze into the face of Jesus Christ.

2 CORINTHIANS 4:6

Just as God spoke light into existence in the beginning of creation, so God has made us come alive in the light of Christ. We have been born again by the radiant mercy of his power at work within us. Through spiritual revelation, we are able to see what we could not understand before. In Christ, what once was hidden has come to light.

The apostles were face-to-face with the King of Glory in all of his humanity. Jesus Christ experienced the totality of the human experience, and yet he did not sin. He became the door through whom we enter the fullness of the presence of God. As we gaze on his glory through fellowship with his Spirit, we become beacons of his light to the world.

Jesus, thank you for the light of your presence. There are no shadows in you, and I know that I can trust your incomparable wisdom. Shine through my life as I set my gaze on you.

Carriers of God's Glory

We are like common clay jars that carry this glorious treasure within, so that this immeasurable power will be seen as God's, not ours.

2 CORINTHIANS 4:7

We are vessels of God's glory, and we are carriers of his presence. As we continually submit to his leadership, he powerfully moves through our yielded lives with beautiful miracles of mercy. When we are weak, the grace of God strengthens us from the inside out. When we are empty, he fills us up with himself.

Our world glorifies the stories of people who rise from the ashes by sheer force of will. But the truth is, we don't have to be superheroes of our stories to experience the power of God. The mercy of God does not rely on our strength. It is not bound by our abilities. When we are weak, he is strong. When we are beaten down, he is our comfort. He is the goodness. He will always be our goodness. What a reason to rejoice today.

Great God, my simple life contains a great treasure and power only because of you. I yield to you, knowing that there is superior satisfaction in your presence and in your affection. Fill me up with more of you.

In Light of Eternity

We view our slight, short-lived troubles in the light of eternity.
We see our difficulties as the substance that produces for us
an eternal, weighty glory far beyond all comparison.

2 CORINTHIANS 4:17

When the days are long and our hearts grow weary, may we not give up. Paul says in verse 16, even though our bodies may wear down, our inner beings can be renewed every single day. That means today we have opportunity for renewal. Every moment is a chance to experience the relief and reviving power of God through his Spirit.

No matter the troubles we face, what lies ahead of us in the eternal kingdom of Christ is far better than anything we leave behind. No matter the successes we experience, their joy will pale in comparison to the pure joy of living in Christ's presence for eternity. He will be our sun, and we will see everything clearly. We will know him in fullness, and every tear will be wiped from our eyes. Pain will be but a memory. Let's take courage, then, and look to the hope that awaits us and continue to persevere here and now.

Jesus, I long for the incomparable joy of knowing you fully even as I am fully known. Revive my hope in your promises and minister to my heart with your presence.

Higher Perspective

We don't focus our attention on what is seen but on what is unseen.
For what is seen is temporary, but the unseen realm is eternal.

2 CORINTHIANS 4:18

When we spend our time overly focused on the trivial matters of life, we can get tunnel vision. Unable to see the beauty and mystery that is still present in the world around us, we only see the things that feel burdensome and overwhelming. Though this is a very human thing to do, there are ways that we can train our brains to see different possibilities.

When we get curious in the present moment, bringing our attention to things we normally overlook, we are able to ground ourselves. When we take a new way home, explore a new road, city, or are exposed to different cultures, customs, and languages, we are able to recognize that there is more to life than our little corners of the world can contain. How much more, then, awaits us in the unseen realm of Christ's glorious kingdom. May we set our priorities straight as we value the ways of his kingdom, the fruit of his Spirit, and the incomparable goodness of his fellowship.

Wonderful One, may I be caught up in the awe of who you are even as I recognize your fingerprints in the world around me. I look for you.

Guaranteed Hope

This is no empty hope, for God himself is the one who has prepared us for this wonderful destiny. And to confirm this promise, he has given us the Holy Spirit, like an engagement ring, as a guarantee.

2 CORINTHIANS 5:5

As we live by faith in this world, we are not the arbitrators of our hope. God himself is our hope. In him, we have the guarantee of eternal life. He is the one who has done the work to prepare us for our wonderful destiny in his kingdom. It is *his* work, and we are his workmanship.

Let go of the responsibility to be and do it all perfectly today. You have the Spirit of God as your help in all things. Lean into the presence of God and ask for what you need. Rely on him for wisdom, for support, and for guidance. When you are stumped, take your problems to him. He will surely give you the peace of his presence; his solutions are full of simple wisdom and clarity. He is trustworthy. You can bet your life on him.

Spirit, I want to trust you more than I do my own logic. I know that there is purpose in everything you do, and I know that not all that happens in the world is your work. Refresh my hope in you today!

Longing for More

That's why we're always full of courage. Even while we're at home in the body, we're homesick to be with the Master—for we live by faith, not by what we see with our eyes.

2 CORINTHIANS 5:6–7

Do you relate to Paul's statement here? Do you know what it is to long for more than you've experienced yet in this life? Have you tasted and seen the goodness of God, and yet you long for more than you've known? We are all built for eternity. That is why goodbyes are so hard. We were meant for fellowship, belonging, and peace.

As long as we are living in this world, longings will continue to drive us. All our longings are satisfied in Christ, and yet we are only getting glimpses here and there. We're homesick for a land that we have not yet known. We're lovesick for our Savior and our Father. Let us, then, continue to live by faith for what we cannot yet see fully. We are on our way.

Redeemer, I long for the day when I will see you face-to-face. I yearn for the physical touch of your arms wrapped around me. I cannot wait for that day. And yet, knowing there is more ahead, I persevere in faith now. Meet me with fresh mercy in your presence today.

June

Driving Ambition

Whether we live or die we make it our life's passion
to live our lives pleasing to him.

2 CORINTHIANS 5:9

What a peace it is to know that when we pass from this body, we enter into the eternal kingdom of Christ that knows no end. Our spirits live on, and we will be clothed in new bodies, just as Christ resurrected in his imperishable body.

Are we so focused on tasks that we forget the joys of living? Are we so focused on living that we avoid the eternal hope that awaits us when our mortal bodies fail? May we live with the pure motive of love behind everything we do. As we do, our lives bring honor and glory to God, who is love incarnate. Let this be our driving ambition—to live with integrity, kindness, and peace. Let's be people who radiate the mercy of Christ through our surrendered lives.

Jesus, I won't avoid the path of your unfailing love that leads me to lay down my own opinions and consider the well-being of others. I don't try to do this on my own, but I rely on your Spirit to fill me, transform me, and expand my understanding as I live it out.

Seized by Love

It is Christ's love that fuels our passion and holds us tightly, because we are convinced that he has given his life for all of us.

2 CORINTHIANS 5:14

When Christ's love fills our hearts, it becomes the motivating passion of our lives. What choice do we have but to surrender everything to God? He has given us *everything* that he has. He laid down his own life, not thinking of himself as too precious to offer to us. His love moved him to set aside all that he had in the Father's presence to liberate us and show us the way to know God in Spirit and in truth.

What a wonderful Savior! Why would we hold anything back from him? He is motivated by mercy in all that he does, and he provided a way to be free from the curse of sin and death. Why would we choose anything but full liberation in his mercy? There is nothing better in heaven or on earth than his living love.

Christ Jesus, I am undone at the reminder of the lengths you went to save us—to save me. I come alive in your loyal love, and I am free in your presence. I offer you all that I am, for you are worthy and you are trustworthy.

Completely New

Now, if anyone is enfolded into Christ, he has become an entirely new person. All that is related to the old order has vanished. Behold, everything is fresh and new.

2 CORINTHIANS 5:17

What a glorious reality is ours in Christ! He who knew no sin took on ours so that we could be free from its weight. He sets us free in his love, and he makes us entirely new. The old order has vanished. This includes our old identity, our life of sin, the shame we were under, the religious works we did to try to please God, our old mindsets, and more.

As new creations in Christ, we will experience no hindrances to his love. We are not simply reformed or renovated; we are completely new in him. Let us take time to consider the transformation we have undergone in his mercy. What has he liberated us from? What did we used to do that we no longer have the urge to do? Let's give him praise for all that he has done and thank him for all that he is continuing to do in us.

Lord Jesus, thank you for covering me completely in your mercy. I am new in you. Thank you for the complete freedom I have found in you.

Seize the Moment

For he says,
I listened to you at the time of my favor.
And the day when you needed salvation,
I came to your aid.
So can't you see?
Now is the time to respond to his favor!
Now is the day of salvation!

2 CORINTHIANS 6:2

The marvelous grace of God is a free gift to those who will receive it. Do we take hold of what is offered to us? Let's not take his grace for granted, as Paul expresses in the previous verse. The grace of God empowers us to be transformed in the mercy of God.

Today is the day of salvation—that is always true! Let's not put off until tomorrow what we can seize today. The abundance of God's kingdom is available to us through his Spirit. He is ready and waiting for our response to his invitation. What more is the Lord inviting you into today? Take time to listen to his voice and respond to him.

Jesus, thank you for your help whenever I call on you. I don't want to waste a moment thinking that I can do better on my own than in partnership with you. I rely on you, Lord. Meet me, speak your living words of life over me, and move in mighty ways as I respond to you.

In Every Season

We may suffer, yet in every season we are always found rejoicing.
We may be poor, yet we bestow great riches on many.
We seem to have nothing, yet in reality we possess all things.

2 CORINTHIANS 6:10

Though we cannot avoid pain and suffering in our lives, we can cultivate fellowship with the Spirit through it all. His grace fuels our gratitude. His nearness brings us joy. His mercy breathes hope into our hearts.

We don't have to wait until we are in a worry-free space to offer what we already have in service to God. We don't have to wait until chaos calms in our lives in order to rejoice in the present help of God. In every season of the soul, there is fullness in Christ. In every moment, there is hope, faith, and love. Even when we suffer, may we be found rejoicing in the beauty of fellowship with our wonderfully kind Savior.

Comforter, you are my reason for rejoicing in every season and every trial. I will not give up looking to you for help and for hope. Fill me up with your love and revive my weary heart in you.

Make Room

I speak to you as our children.
Make room in your hearts for us
as we have done for you.

2 CORINTHIANS 6:13

W hen we live with open-hearted surrender to the Lord and his love, we allow for our hearts to expand in compassion toward others as well. As he guides us in the incomparable goodness of his fellowship, we cannot avoid our how lives intersect with those he passionately pursues with loving-kindness.

In the family of God, there is room for all. Christ calls the outcasts as well as the notable into his kingdom. He does not turn away any who turn to him for help. His mercy reaches everyone. We cannot call ourselves followers of Christ and act in any other way. We cannot pick and choose whom God loves, and we should not act in favoritism. May we extend mercy in the same measure to all of God's children, for he loves us all in the same unimaginable measure.

Father, thank you for your love that does not show favoritism. You don't value the same things that society does. Power does not impress you, and neither does a polished life. I want to reflect your living love in the way that I relate to all. Transform my heart in your mercy.

He Knows

> God, who always knows how to encourage the depressed,
> encouraged us greatly by the arrival of Titus.
>
> 2 CORINTHIANS 7:6

How did Titus encourage the apostles? Paul goes on to say in verse 7, "We were relieved…because of the report he brought us of how you refreshed his heart." One person's encouragement can be the relief of others. Have you ever experienced joy and hope because of someone else's testimony of goodness?

Our lives are interconnected. We cannot go through life as isolated islands, unaffected by the decisions, attitudes, and choices of those around us. Relationships are among our greatest gifts in this life. Through companionship, we experience the beauty of knowing and being known, loved, and accepted. God knows exactly what we need when we need it. Let's rejoice in the relief we find through the encouragement of others.

God, you always know how to encourage our hearts. You know exactly what I need, and I trust that you will provide for what my heart longs for today. I lean into you and into the gift of friendship.

The Gift of Godly Sorrow

Now I'm overjoyed—not because I made you sad, but because your grief led you to a deep repentance. You experienced godly sorrow, and as God intended, it brought about gain for you, not loss, so that no harm has been done by us.

2 CORINTHIANS 7:9

Sorrow for our sins is not something that we need to escape or run from. It is a meaningful response within our hearts to the realization that we have caused someone else pain. When we fail others, apathy does not serve anyone, including ourselves. When we realize that we have hurt someone, the appropriate response is to acknowledge what we have done. Let's be people who let our realizations sink deeper than the surface of our thoughts.

Paul says that godly sorrow is a gift. When we have the deep realization that we have gotten it wrong in one way or another, grief has the opportunity to lead us to repentance. Repentance is a turning of our hearts toward restoration in Christ. We don't just admit our wrongs, but we also resolve to make them right and to change our patterns through the grace of God.

Lord, I don't want to run from the difficult emotion of godly sorrow or even regret. When it comes up, instead of turning away from it, I will turn toward it and invite your love to restore me and transform me in your living love.

Victorious Repentance

God designed us to feel remorse over sin in order to produce
repentance that leads to victory. This leaves us with no regrets.
But the sorrow of the world works death.

2 CORINTHIANS 7:10

Most of us experience remorse over our sin. Our conscience
keeps us from continually hurting others when we are
made aware how our behavior negatively affects them. When we
admit our wrongs, humbly ask forgiveness, and seek restoration,
we choose to walk in the way of Christ. Pride keeps us from admitting our failures while humility advises us to admit our faults.

Is there a person or situation in your life where you are aware
of the hurt you have caused but have not repented? Today is the
day to walk into the victory of repentance. Turn away from your
sin, turn toward God, and admit your failure. Make it right with
those you have the opportunity to. Reach out, express your regret,
and ask forgiveness. Let love lead you out of your comfort zone.
Peace will meet you there as you rely on God's leadership.

*Worthy One, I am not too proud to admit when I have been wrong.
I not only look to you for restoration, but I will go further and seek
forgiveness from those I have wronged. I know that this is your way.*

Supernatural Joy

Even during a season of severe difficulty, tremendous suffering,
and extreme poverty, their super-abundant joy overflowed
into an act of extravagant generosity.

2 CORINTHIANS 8:2

In describing the grace that God had poured out on the churches of Macedonia, Paul highlighted the response of the people. Their reaction to the joy of the Lord among them was to become people of extravagant generosity. They looked for ways to support and help fellow believers who were living in poverty.

Joy leads to generosity. How have you seen this displayed in your life? As you experience the abundance of supernatural joy in God's presence, look for ways to share with others who have less than you. How can you encourage someone today? Look for little ways to sacrifice a momentary pleasure for yourself while looking to bring relief to someone else. There are a million different ways to do this. Let joy lead you.

Joyful Jehovah, fill me up with the supernatural joy of your presence today regardless of the challenges I face or the trials I walk through. As your joy as my source, I will look for ways to gleefully give to others.

Growth in Generosity

You do well and excel in every respect—in unstoppable faith, in powerful preaching, in revelation knowledge, in your passionate devotion, and in sharing the love we have shown to you. So make sure that you also excel in grace-filled generosity.

2 CORINTHIANS 8:7

There are several features of godliness outlined in this verse. As believers and followers of Christ, may we excel in everything, have unstoppable faith, have an anointing of grace to speak the Word, have revelation knowledge, live in passionate devotion, and show love. On top of all this, let us not forget to be generous.

Does this seem too lofty a list to achieve? It is all by God's grace, not our own perfection. It is not a laundry list of items that we need to run down every day, but a series of values to align our hearts with. Look at the attributes laid out and focus on one to grow in today. Be mindful throughout your day, praying for grace to choose over and over again the way of Christ.

Loving Lord, it is only by your grace that I do anything well. I want to grow in generosity of heart, attention, time, and resources. May your love fuel my choices today.

Extravagant Grace

You have experienced the extravagant grace of our Lord Jesus Christ, that although he was infinitely rich, he impoverished himself for our sake, so that by his poverty, we become rich beyond measure.

2 CORINTHIANS 8:9

The way of the cross is not a series of orders to follow but a path of living love that empowers us to choose Christ over every other thing. His grace inspires us in ways that we would not naturally be inclined. It enables us to lay down our own rights in order to help others.

This is what Christ did for us. He laid down his own life in order to give us eternal life. He is our Savior, and he did not count himself as too worthy to stoop to dust and earth. If we truly want to be more like him, then we will follow his standard. We won't hold too tightly to our own comfort, our ideals, or our resources. When we see others in need, we will reach out and offer them from our own abundance. This is the way of grace.

Gracious Christ, thank you for your beautiful example of laid-down-love. I don't want to be so lulled by my comfort that I refuse to help others when I am able or hold back from sacrificing when it is inconvenient. Give me grace as I choose your way.

Finish Strong

You should finish what you started. You were so eager in your intentions to give, so go do it. Finish this act of worship according to your ability to give.

2 CORINTHIANS 8:11

I t is easy to start almost anything strong and with good intentions. In the nitty-gritty of life, though, our intentions may fall flat as the luster of new beginnings gives way to the messy middle. Wherever you find yourself in the process, may you find renewed encouragement to keep going.

Finishing strong is a discipline, not something that happens by chance. Motivation helps, but it is not necessary to follow through on our commitments. Motivation will come and go, but it is on us to choose to do what we said we would every step of the way. We can do what we need to do unmotivated. And God will meet us with grace to help us persevere until we are at the finish line.

Faithful One, I don't want to be known as a fickle person. I want my word to matter. I will make sure to give my yeses to those things that I intend on following through on. Give me grace-strength to keep going and to do what I set out to.

Mindful Sharing

Your surplus could meet their need,
and their abundance may one day meet your need.
This equal sharing of abundance will mean a fair balance.

2 CORINTHIANS 8:14

This text to the Corinthian church lays out principles for giving, and these principles hold true today. A willing and cheerful offering is more important than the amount that you give. Financial commitments should be taken seriously. We are to share what we have with those in need with the awareness that the time may come when we will need their help.

Our giving doesn't just reflect our own generosity but also our devotion to Christ. We should give what we are able to give and not stress about what we cannot offer. We are also to give in proportion to our income. With all these things in mind, consider how your giving measures up. Take some time in the presence of the Lord and ask him to speak his truth over your circumstances.

Jesus, I invite your voice of wisdom to instruct me in my giving. Show me where I am doing well and where I have room to grow. I want to reflect your extravagant mercy in every way possible.

Check Your Heart

Here's my point. A stingy sower will reap a meager harvest, but the one who sows from a generous spirit will reap an abundant harvest.

2 CORINTHIANS 9:6

Generosity is a virtue. It is a beautiful reflection of God's mercy toward us. He gives unceasingly from the abundance of his kingdom, and we receive as empty vessels the overflowing riches of his love. Why would we hoard what we have, refusing to share with others, when we claim to want to be like Christ?

May we be found as lovers of God with our lives as much and even more than with our mouths. A thousand worship services full of songs of praise pale in comparison to a life lived outside of the walls of a church building with the visible laid-down-love of Christ. Let's be people who live our love out loud with our actions. What a pleasing offering that is to God.

Generous One, your mercy is so abundant that no one can measure it. I won't be stingy with the gifts you have given me. I will share freely today in ways that matter in my community.

Fountain of Joy

Let giving flow from your heart,
not from a sense of religious duty.
Let it spring up freely from the joy of giving—
all because God loves hilarious generosity!

2 CORINTHIANS 9:7

What is your picture of God? Is it of an overly serious figure that doles out his grace and mercy begrudgingly? Is it of a somber grandfatherly man who does not particularly like people but puts up with them, in any case, because he created them? Perhaps you imagine him more like the father of the prodigal son, full of hope and longing, full of love ready to fully restore his sons and daughters who turn toward him?

Jesus told the parable of the prodigal son so that we would know better what the Father is like. He runs to meet us on the path, long before we have made our way to his house. He wraps us up in robes of righteousness, throwing a celebration for our homecoming. There are no lectures, only tears of joy. In his joy, we find relief. In our relief, we are filled with joy in return.

Lord, I want to live from the joy of your favor. I know all it takes is turning to you. You are incomparably good, irrepressibly merciful, and you cover my shame with your own robes of righteousness.

Overwhelmingly Satisfying

Yes, God is more than ready to overwhelm you with every form of grace, so that you will have more than enough of everything— every moment and in every way. He will make you overflow with abundance in every good thing you do.

2 CORINTHIANS 9:8

The ones who trust in the Lord have no need to worry about what tomorrow will bring. They give to the poor and sow extravagantly as the Lord has set out for them to do, for it is their pleasure to partner with God in generosity. They live with kindness and compassion, helping others.

There is more than enough in the great grace of God to satisfy us in every way imaginable. The more we give, the more God fills us up. This is a kingdom principle. He does not let us run dry. Every time we turn to God, he is more than ready to overwhelm us with every form of grace. Why would we choose to live small, stingy lives when he is inviting us into the great expanse of his kingdom that never depletes?

Gracious God, you are the only one who can truly satisfy my soul. I try not to look for satisfaction in my life though I get beautiful glimpses of your beauty in it. You are the only perfect God, and you are my source of pure joy, hope, peace, and love.

A Better Portion

You will be abundantly enriched in every way as you give generously
on every occasion, for when we take your gifts to those in need,
it causes many to give thanks to God.

2 CORINTHIANS 9:11

When we are in a place to financially sow into others without a thought for our own well-being, we are able to expand our generosity. It is the responsibility of every believer to be generous though what this looks like in each of our lives depends on our unique situation.

Have your circumstances changed? Do you have more resources than you used to? If this is the case, think about your level of giving. Has this also changed? Have you generously expanded how much and how widely you sow into those in need of support? The principle remains the same: each should give what they have determined in their hearts to give. Perhaps spend some time evaluating how that plays out in your life as it is now—not how it was months, years, or even decades ago.

Great God, as I look at my giving, will you move in my heart as to what needs to be adjusted in light of my life and in light of what you are doing? Thank you.

Thought Patterns

We can demolish every deceptive fantasy that opposes God and break through every arrogant attitude that is raised up in defiance of the true knowledge of God. We capture, like prisoners of war, every thought and insist that it bow in obedience to the Anointed One.

2 CORINTHIANS 10:5

Not every thought we think is right. Not every thought is true. Not every thought is reflective of our belief systems. Do we believe everything that pops into our mind? If so, then we are doing ourselves a disservice by not allowing thought patterns that don't reflect truth to raise our suspicions.

We can take our thoughts captive, evaluating them in the light of Christ's truth. His mercy shines a light on the each one, exposing them for what they are. Some mindsets we have carried with us our whole lives through conditioning in our families, cultures, and religious systems. This does not mean that they are based in truth. Let's be active in our pursuit of Christ and in the growth of our inner lives of our hearts, minds, and souls.

Jesus, shine the light of your wisdom and truth on the lies that I have believed about myself, others, you, and the world. I won't just believe what I've thought; I will put it before you, and if it doesn't line up, I will let it go.

Unashamed

I am not ashamed, even if I've come across as one who has overstated the authority given to us by the Lord. For it is the authority to help build you up, not tear you down.

2 CORINTHIANS 10:8

We cannot control how others perceive us, nor can we manage what they think of us. The only will we can truly affect is our own. Let's take agency over our own lives and choices and leave to others what they want to think of us. If they choose to express their thoughts to us, then we can handle that accordingly. But we do no one any good when we jump to conclusions about what others think about us.

Trying to manage another person's internal world is wasted energy. It does nothing for them or for us. Let's instead live as unashamed friends of God, walking his path of surrendered love. If we are living with integrity in the light of his mercy, then we have nothing to be embarrassed about. The Lord is our leader, and it's his opinion of us that matters the most.

Lord God, you are the audience I live for. Where I have inflated others' opinions of me, I surrender it to you. Give me a revelation of your thoughts of me. Who do you say I am?

Confidence in Christ

The one who boasts must boast in the Lord.
So let's be clear. To have the Lord's approval and commendation
is of greater value than bragging about oneself.

2 CORINTHIANS 10:17–18

There is no greater approval we will ever find in this life than in the commendation of God over our lives. By his grace, he offers us acceptance without condition. He gathers us into his arms as beloved children. He builds us up in his love and sends us out in his image. Christ is our confidence, full stop. He is the foundation we build our lives upon.

It is good to put our hands to work to reach goals in this life. Ambition is not a bad thing. Yet everything that we accomplish in this world pales in comparison to the power of God's mercy as displayed through Christ. We don't stop living when we are in Christ. We live surrendered to and emboldened by his Spirit working in us.

Lord Jesus, I celebrate your work in my life. I am thankful for your mercy, peace, and joy woven through the threads of my story. Keep doing what you do as I walk hand in hand with you.

Treasure of Revelation Knowledge

Although I may not be a polished or eloquent speaker, I'm certainly not an amateur in revelation knowledge. Indeed, we have demonstrated this to you time and again.

2 CORINTHIANS 11:6

Some people have a natural charisma that draws others in. Paul did not have this, and he is up front about it. At the same time, someone's charisma does not necessarily reflect their character. Just as we cannot judge a book by its cover, so also we cannot presume that someone who talks a good talk is more qualified in Christ than any other.

We all have different gifts and talents. But wisdom remains the same. The values of Christ's kingdom never change. We do not have to be polished vessels in order to be used by God. Have you fallen into the trap of comparison? Have you disqualified your own voice or the voice of others because of the package it comes in? The treasure of revelation knowledge is available to all who seek the Lord. If you give yourself to anything, let it be to knowing Christ more. He is accessible.

Gracious King, I'm so thankful to know you and be known by you. You are my exceedingly great reward. Meet me with your living love and expand my understanding in your revelation knowledge today.

God's Work

> If boasting is necessary,
> I will boast about examples of my weakness.
>
> 2 CORINTHIANS 11:30

People seem to be impressed with accomplishments, accolades, and endorsements. Yet, in the kingdom of Christ, none of it matters. Paul dismisses the thought that these things are of lasting value to those who follow Christ. He instead flips the script and begins to boast about his weakness. Perhaps he was just trying to make a point. Regardless, he turns the attention back to Christ and his grace.

It is the grace of God that empowers us in our weakness. When we have nothing to offer Christ, he fills us with his Spirit and empowers us with his own strength. We lean on him in all things, for he is our source. He meets our needs, he heals our diseases, and he satisfies our souls. He is our help in times of need. Let's boast about how he has delivered us in our weakness.

Miracle Maker, you are the God who turns ashes into a garden of your glory. Your mercy turns my weakness into a testimony of your goodness. I rely on you. I will boast of you so that I remember who you are and what you have done.

More Than Enough

He answered me, "My grace is always more than enough for you, and my power finds its full expression through your weakness." So I will celebrate my weaknesses, for when I'm weak I sense more deeply the mighty power of Christ living in me.

2 CORINTHIANS 12:9

God answered Paul's plea for removal of a "thorn in his flesh" by saying that his grace is more than enough for him. God will not always take away our problem, but he will always give us his abundant grace to help us through it. His power finds full expression through our weakness.

What thorn are you dealing with? Know this: God is with you in it. He has not abandoned you, and he has not ignored your cries for help. Listen closely to what he is speaking over your heart today. How close is his grace? How abundant is his mercy? Join Paul in celebrating your weakness and lean into the power of Christ living in you.

Spirit of God, you are my living hope and my strength when I have none. Rise up within me and encourage me in your presence. I need you in my weakness.

What a Delight

I'm not defeated by my weakness, but delighted! For when I feel my weakness and endure mistreatment—when I'm surrounded with troubles on every side and face persecution because of my love for Christ—I am made yet stronger. For my weakness becomes a portal to God's power.

2 CORINTHIANS 12:10

Everything we endure in this life is an invitation. Sometimes the things that happen to us have reasons that are too complex for us to understand, but we do not need to find underlying meaning in every one of our circumstances. Even still, there is an invitation at every opportunity for surrender in Christ to trust God in his faithfulness. God turns our disappointments into victory songs.

As we delight in our weaknesses, we find that they become portals to God's power at work within us. As we release the fight against discomfort and the unknown, we are able to grab hold of the grace of God at hand. Let's let go of the struggle and trust the one who holds us close.

Gracious Father, teach me how to use the pain in my life as a portal to your merciful presence. Move in me, through me, and receive glory through my surrendered weakness.

Robed with Power

> Although he was crucified as a "weakling," now he lives robed with God's power. And we also are "weak ones" in our co-crucifixion with him, but now we live in God's triumphant power together with him.
>
> 2 CORINTHIANS 13:4

There is no question that we each face struggles in this life. But we are not victims in these struggles. Paul says in 2 Corinthians 13:3, "Christ is not weak or feeble in his dealings with you but mighty and powerful within you." His Spirit is at home in those of us who have surrendered our hearts and lives to him. To say that we are slaves to our sin is to say that Christ is helpless within us.

We know that this is not true. We know that Christ is robed with God's power. We, too, are living in God's triumphant power with Christ. Let's not give away our power so easily, then, with excuses for our bad behavior. If we truly want to live in freedom, we won't give the power of our lives to any but Christ. It is his power that liberates us.

Christ, I am covered by your mercy robes. Break the power of sin, shame, and fear over my life as I submit to you. By your grace, I won't willingly come under cycles that keep me stuck any more.

Hold Steady

Now your souls will be strengthened and healed if you hold steadfast to your faith. Haven't you already experienced Jesus Christ himself living in you? If not, you are deficient.

2 CORINTHIANS 13:5

The life of a follower of Christ is not passive. Life is full of twists and turns, competing interests and ideologies, and shifting experiences. The world's focus changes often. The extreme voices get further apart and louder at each end. May we not be found shouting platitudes at one another, but by meeting each other with love and willingness to understand in the middle. This is where we help shoulder each other's burdens. This is where love is lived out.

We are made stronger in the family of faith, united under Christ's leadership. May we hold steadfast to Christ, to his kingdom values and ways, in faith. Let us lean on the support of others when we need to be encouraged, and let's reach out to others when we see they are in need. Holding steady is not staying fixed in a pinpointed place but rather remaining in the flowing river of God's love as we journey through this life.

Jesus, your life is the foundation of my understanding of love. Work your power in my life as I remain connected to you, my Vine and the keeper of my soul.

Flawless

We pray to God that you will be flawless, not to validate our ministry among you but so that you may continue on the path of righteousness even if we are denigrated.

2 CORINTHIANS 13:7

The poetic declaration of King Solomon to his bride in Song of Songs 4:7 says, "Every part of you is so beautiful, my darling. Perfect is your beauty, without flaw within." This is what Christ says over us, his bride. We are covered in the robes of his righteousness, claimed as his very own, without flaw.

Paul wanted the church at Corinth to continue in righteousness more than he wanted others to perceive him as a good leader or teacher. Are we more concerned with our reputations or the growth of others in the liberating truth of Christ? He frees us and calls us pure in the life-giving light of his mercy. May we live free from the shackles of our fear, passionately pursuing him in every area of our lives.

Christ, in your love I have been declared flawless. It is in that liberating confidence that I want to remain all my days. Purify me in your mercy and lead me on in your gracious wisdom. Where you lead, I will follow.

Unmistakable Love

> Now, may the grace and joyous favor of the Lord Jesus Christ,
> the unambiguous love of God, and the precious communion
> that we share in the Holy Spirit be yours continually. Amen!
>
> 2 CORINTHIANS 13:14

This statement was the closing benediction of Paul's second letter to the Corinthian church. His final prayer over them encourages them (and us) to remain covered in the grace of God, the jubilant favor of Jesus Christ, and the unequivocal love of God. He also highlights the communion we find in fellowship with the Holy Spirit—and that it can be our continual and precious experience.

As you go about your day, may the unmistakable love of God rise up to meet you. May the generous grace of God empower you to continue to choose to follow Christ's kingdom ways. As you submit to his leadership, may you know the joy of his communion and unmatched wisdom. Go in the peace of your God, and feast on the fellowship of the Holy Spirit with you.

Holy Spirit, meet me in the details of my day. Break through the fog of my thoughts and bring clarity to my confusion. Shine the light of your love on my heart and encourage my hope in your overwhelming power.

All That Is

May God's undeserved kindness and total well-being that flow from our Father God and from the Lord Jesus be yours. He's the Anointed One who offered himself as the sacrifice for our sins! He has rescued us from this evil world system and set us free, just as our Father God desired.

GALATIANS 1:3–4

The *well-being* that flows from God is from the word *peace*. Peace is much more than a calm state without conflict. In the Hebraic mindset, peace equates to health, prosperity, peace, and total well-being. Paul uses this greeting many times over in his various letters.

Undeserved kindness is the epitome of God's grace and mercy. All that God has, he bestows on us in Christ. Without restraint, without complaint or condition, he offers us the limitless affection of his heart. He covers us in his peace and righteousness, and he fills us with hope, faith, and love. Everything in this world has its origin in the Father. Every good gift is from his hand. May we be open vessels, willing to receive all that he pours out.

Jesus, I am a container of your glory. Fill me up with the goodness of your presence through your Spirit. Pour into me, over me, and through me. I am yours.

July

Supreme Passion

My supreme passion is to please God. For if all I attempt to do
is please people, I would fail to be a true servant of Christ.

GALATIANS 1:10

The message of the gospel of Christ does not change through the ages. We can better understand his message through the context of the times, but there is no adding or subtracting from God's grace poured out to us through the all-sufficient sacrifice of Christ. His resurrection power is still the same grave-busting power today. His love is still the standard. Faith in Jesus Christ as Redeemer has not become obsolete.

Do we spend more time trying to appease others than we do obeying what Christ has clearly spoken to us? Do we look for ways to remain comfortable in our communities, or do we allow the love of God to draw us out beyond our fences? His compassion is always active, not stagnant. May Christ be our supreme passion, and may his opinion be the one that matters the most.

Savior, I fix my eyes on you today. I refocus my attention on who you are and what you have said, and I submit to your path of love that leads me out of self-preservation. You are worth it, and my life is enriched by you.

Transformed by Christ

The only thing they heard about me was this:
"Our former enemy, who once brutally persecuted us,
is now preaching the good news of the faith that he tried to destroy!"

GALATIANS 1:23

Paul's conversion was no ordinary change in his life. He was a Pharisee—he knew the law of Moses better than most, and he was a persecutor of the early church. He was passionate about his religion, and he believed what he was doing to be right. It was God's power that encountered him and transformed his life.

The extreme revolution in Paul's personal life astounded the early church. When the followers of Christ heard that he was now preaching the gospel of the good news, they were overjoyed. Instead of being skeptical of those who have changed their minds from what they once believed, may we rejoice with those whose lives are transformed in the living love of Christ. The transformative power of the Spirit is accessible to each of us.

Spirit of Christ, thank you for the ways that you transform the lives of your people. Keep moving and keep working. I rejoice with your people in your power.

Reason to Praise

Because of the transformation that took place in my life,
they praised God even more!

GALATIANS 1:24

Have you ever witnessed a positive transformation in someone's life? Maybe you have watched someone struggle with
addiction and come out on the other side. Perhaps you have seen
someone blossom into themselves after being really insecure.
There are some transformations that, with grit and determina-
tion, can be experienced. There are others, though, that are by the
grace and power of God alone.

Nothing is impossible for God. The same God who encountered Paul on the road to Damascus and set him on a journey of
powerful conversion is the same God who moves in miracles of
mercy today. The same power that raised Christ from the dead is
working in us still. Every life that is transformed in the mercy of
God is a reason to praise the Lord even more. These transformed
lives add fuel to the fire of our passion.

*Jesus, I praise you for the powerful ways you transform those who
look to you. Remind me of my own experiences as well as those
experiences of the ones I love, and I will offer you more praise today.*

Freedom in Grace

You must know that we did not submit to their religious shackles,
not even for a moment, so that we might keep the truth of the
gospel of grace unadulterated for you.

GALATIANS 2:5

The gospel of grace is explicit about our freedom in Christ.
There are no religious shackles in the liberating love of Jesus.
We should be wary of those who look to micromanage our faith
with their rules and regulations. If we are living by the mercy of
God, serving God in humility and others with compassion, then
what God does not condemn, let's not let another condemn in us.

The freedom of Christ is not fickle, and it is not fragile. We
can truly trust the power of God's mercy in our lives. We come
alive in the power of his love, and his joy, peace, and steadfast
presence keep us close to him. The correction of God is laced with
kindness, but the condemnation of religious know-it-alls is full of
shame. Let's remain free in the unadulterated grace of God and
not give in to the fear tactics of those who are less concerned with
Christ and more concerned with their own influence.

Gracious God, thank you for the freedom I have in you. Keep me
free from the burdens others would place on me that you do not.
Thank you.

Entrusted by God

Even those most influential among the brothers were not able to add anything to my message. Who they are before men makes no difference to me, for God is not impressed by their reputations.

GALATIANS 2:6

When we are walking in the light of God's loving truth, we don't need to fear the disapproval of others, nor do we need to be preoccupied with the favor of anyone but God. Paul's message was the fullness of the gospel. When we align our lives in the gospel of grace, we are free from the burden of pleasing others.

The kingdom of God is governed by the values of Christ. It is not a list of dos and don'ts. It is wonderfully diverse, full of the expressions of every language and culture. Why should we be so concerned with blending in when God has freed us up to be uniquely and fully ourselves? As long as we follow the law of love and the lead of Christ, we are on the right path.

Merciful Lord, thank you for the reminder that I am unique and still wholly yours. I want to walk in the liberty of your love without being preoccupied by what others think. Your opinion is the one that matters the most.

Something to Remember

They simply requested one thing of me: that I would remember the poor and needy, which was the burden I was already carrying in my heart.

GALATIANS 2:10

When Jesus ministered, he often spent time with those who were poor and needy. He healed those whom society ignored. He did not turn away the poor and needy, and neither should we.

How do we remember those in need? How do we help them? How do we support systems that benefit them? Part of the purpose of the church is to be the hands and feet of Jesus, providing for the needs of those less fortunate. How can we help lift up those who have been beaten down by the world and offer them a place of respite, rest, and restoration? May we keep this in mind as we go about our lives, looking for ways to implement this truth.

Prince of Peace, you are the supreme example of living love. You are the image of powerful mercy. May I reflect you as I look for ways to help those in my community. Empower me in your grace with solutions and, more than that, a willing heart full of compassion.

Through Faith Alone

We know that no one receives God's perfect righteousness as a reward for keeping the law, but only by the faith of Jesus, the Messiah! His faithfulness has saved us, and we have received God's perfect righteousness. Now we know that God accepts no one by the keeping of religious laws!

GALATIANS 2:16

We cannot earn the grace of God, and we cannot convince the Father to love us more than he already does. When we come to him through Christ, we are covered in the purity and righteousness of Christ himself. Everything that could have been held against us is covered. Christ removes the stain of our sin, and he sets us free in the cleansing power of his mercy.

Why try to earn his favor then? We already have it in Christ. Let's let our faith lead us into greater freedom from obligation. Let's live from the passionate pursuit of love. We have peace with God through Christ our Savior. Nothing else is required. We live in the light of his love all the days of our lives. We are accepted as his children through his choice and through our faith in his faithfulness. Praise God!

Jesus, you are my righteousness. There is nothing else I truly need outside of you. Fill my life with the wonders of your love.

One with Christ

My old identity has been co-crucified with Christ and no longer
lives. And now the essence of this new life is no longer mine, for the
Anointed One lives his life through me—we live in union as one!
My new life is empowered by the faith of the Son of God...
dispensing his life into mine!

GALATIANS 2:20

Just as Paul's old life of persecuting Christians was put away
under Christ, so are the shames of our own pasts. The lives
we lived unto ourselves have been brought under Christ and his
powerful sacrifice. In his resurrection life, we have been given a
fresh chance.

When we live in union with Christ, his merciful power
overcomes our weakness. We are empowered by faith, even in our
weaknesses, and we depend on his life within us to fuel our own
passion. All that we have is from him—even the love we experience toward him finds its origin in his affection over us. Let us,
then, lean on him for all that we need. He has given us clean slates
in his mercy.

*Redeemer, thank you for the power of your resurrection life. What
you do not hold against me any longer, I will no longer hold against
myself. I am free in your love.*

New Beginnings

Your new life began when the Holy Spirit gave you a new birth.
Why then would you so foolishly turn from living in the Spirit
by trying to finish by your own works?

GALATIANS 3:3

Paul makes it clear that keeping the rigor of Jewish laws does not lead to salvation. The Holy Spirit is not a gift to those who earn him. We have been redeemed by the power of God's grace. When we join our faith to his grace, we are empowered to live as vessels of his glory. The Holy Spirit makes itself at home within us.

Are you living by the power of the Spirit or by the qualifications of your own works? Are you depending on God's grace or your own abilities? There is nothing wrong with working hard, but that is not the same thing as striving for a seat at a table where you already have a reserved spot. God has made room for us, and we accept his invitation. What a gloriously generous God he is.

Spirit, thank you for making yourself at home in me. I yield to your leadership, and I will follow your ways. Thank you for the fresh mercy of new beginnings in you.

A Steady Stream

Let me ask you again: What does the lavish supply of the Holy Spirit in your life and the miracles of God's tremendous power have to do with you keeping religious laws? The Holy Spirit is poured out upon us through the revelation and power of faith!

GALATIANS 3:5

Paul had spent his life, up until the miraculous encounter he had on the road to Damascus, keeping the Hebrew religious laws. He knew that following the law of Moses was not the path to salvation. He knew that the power of the Holy Spirit was not contingent upon following the letter of the law.

There is a steady stream of God's Spirit being poured out on those who look to Christ as their Savior. The Holy Spirit is not a reward for strict adherence to religious rules but as a gift to those who put their faith in Jesus as the way to the Father. Let's make sure we don't confuse this. There is more revelation available to us today in the Spirit. Let's submit our hearts in reverence and look to Christ.

Holy Spirit, I'm so glad that you're not a commodity that can be bought, sold, or earned. You are freely bestowed on all who call on the Lord, and you are full of wonder-working power. Hallelujah!

The Simple Gospel

This means that the covenant between God and Abraham was fulfilled in Messiah and cannot be altered…The law, then, doesn't supersede the promise since the royal proclamation was given before the law. If that were the case, it would have nullified what God said to Abraham. We receive all the promises because of the Promised One— not because we keep the law!

GALATIANS 3:17–18

The revelation of grace that saves us is the premise of the promise that God gave Abraham. All we need is faith to believe it. God's promise is unchanging, and he will never add an addendum that we could somehow miss.

Sometimes simplifying is the most clarifying thing we can do in our lives. When we declutter a space, we are able to better appreciate what we have and see the possibilities of what could be. When we simplify our thinking, we lay aside the distracting details that lead us down rabbit holes to nowhere. Where have we complicated our faith?

Messiah, thank you for the reminder that the message of your gospel is simple grace. When I am tempted to add more to it, bring me back to the beauty of your sufficiency.

Set Free by Faith

Until the revelation of faith for salvation was released, the law was a jailer, holding us as prisoners under lock and key until the "faith," which was destined to be revealed, would set us free.

GALATIANS 3:23

No one is immune to sin. "The Scriptures," as Paul says in verse 22, "make it clear that the whole world is imprisoned by sin!" The law points out our failure to live without fault. None of us is perfect, and no one acts out of compassionate mercy all the time—except for God himself. Therefore, we all sin and fall short of the glory of God.

But a better way was revealed through Christ. He broke the chains of sin and shame and tore the veil that kept the presence of God from the people of God. Through faith in Christ, we are set free from the prison of sin. He is our liberator, not our captor. Does the revelation of his rescue in our lives fuel our joy and passion? Let's give him thanks today.

Redeemer, thank you for setting us free in your love. Thank you for that love that did not stop at accusation or death but sacrificed itself so that we could be liberated from our captivity. Thank you.

Fully Immersed

Faith immersed you into Christ, and now you are covered and clothed with his life. And we no longer see each other in our former state—Jew or non-Jew, rich or poor, male or female—because we're all one through our union with Jesus Christ.

GALATIANS 3:27–28

When you look at others, what lens do you see them through? Do you fixate on the differences between you, or do you acknowledge them while still letting love be the unifier? Every person is made in the image of God. Those who look to Christ as their Savior are covered and clothed with his mercy.

May we be people who don't play favorites based on our preferences. The love of Christ doesn't put people into tiers based on their ethnicity, income, or gender. We are all equal before Christ. And yet we know that this is not how the world operates. May we be radical in our devotion to love one another, no matter what. May we be supporters, encouragers, and lifters of one another, listening to those we differ from as closely as those we agree with. Let's come under the banner of Christ's love and be unified as one.

Messiah, thank you for the power of your love that breaks down barriers. Your mercy is unifying.

Redeemed and Restored

All of this was so that he would redeem and set free those held hostage to the law so that we would receive our freedom and a full legal adoption as his children.

GALATIANS 4:5

We can find no greater freedom in this world than what we find in Christ. His love liberates us from our fear and shame. It sets us free from the sin that once kept us stuck in cycles of self-destruction. Love leads us into greater generosity of spirit. It tends to the vulnerable and cares for the sick. Love reaches out beyond its own borders in compassion. It receives those who are weary from war and gives them shelter.

Jesus Christ was the ultimate human manifestation of love, for he was the living expression of the Father. He redeemed us so that we would not be held hostage by anything—not even the religious regulations of Moses. We receive our freedom through faith in his death and resurrection, and we are accepted into his kingdom as God's own children.

Savior, no one's claim to be better than you can hold up to your powerful mercy. You are Redeemer and Restorer, and you are the one I pledge my life to.

True Children of God

So that we would know that we are his true children, God released the
Spirit of Sonship into our hearts—moving us to cry out intimately,
"My Father! My true Father!"

GALATIANS 4:6

A s children of the Most High, we have been ushered into his
kingdom with the relentless love of our Father displayed
through Christ. His Spirit awakens our hearts in his mercy, and
we are loved to life as he pours out the revelation of God's affection within us. We are his beloved children, and he loves us. Not
because of anything we have done but because he is love.

Spend some time in his presence today. Focus on what it
means to be a child of God. Invite his Spirit to reveal what your
identity is in him. Who does he say that you are? What does
he say about you? How does he speak to you? He is tender and
kind. He is confident and gentle. Listen closely and respond as he
moves in your heart.

*Good Father, I long for a fresh revelation of your love toward me.
Show me who I am in you and release the fears that have been
keeping me from seeing you as you truly are.*

Don't Go Back

Now that we truly know him and are intimately known by him, why would we for a moment consider turning back to those weak and feeble principles of religion, as though we were still subject to them?

GALATIANS 4:9

The purpose of the law of Moses was not only to direct the Jewish people in their dealings with each other but also to draw them closer to God. In the new covenant of Christ, our approach to God is on the basis of grace and faith in the blood of Jesus Christ—always. We don't follow a set of rules in order to get close to God. We draw close to him through faith in Christ.

There is something unhealthy that can happen to believers as they grow in their faith. The longer they walk with God, the more they may rely on the conditions of the churches and theologies of their communities and less on the power of grace through the Spirit. We are saved by grace, and we remain close to God by grace. Anything else is extra, not the rule. Don't be bound by religious dogma. Be led by love.

Messiah, your grace will always be enough for me. It is more than enough. Forgive me for where I have lost sight of my reliance on you and give me your wisdom to walk in your ways with love as my covering.

Willingness to Listen

Beloved ones, I plead with you, brothers and sisters,
become like me, for I became like you.
You did me no wrong.

GALATIANS 4:12

Paul makes an appeal to the Galatians that they would remember how he came to them and that they would try to understand where he was coming from. Distance can remove our filter of grace and love if we are not careful. We can become so preoccupied by the opinions of those around us that we forget how much we respected those who seem easy to ridicule from a distance.

Let's humble our hearts in the mercy of God today, taking care to not dehumanize or degrade those in the family of God. May we be clothed in compassion, listening to understand and not just waiting for an opening to be heard. May we be people who humbly love each other, and may we test the fruit of our beliefs against the mercy we display toward one another.

Spirit, you never miss a thing. Reveal areas in my heart and mindsets where I have strayed from your compassion. Refresh my vision in the purity of your mercy. I yield to you.

Remaining Free

At last we have freedom, for Christ has set us free!
We must always cherish this truth and firmly refuse
to go back into the bondage of our past.

GALATIANS 5:1

If you embrace the truth, it will release true freedom into your
lives." Jesus' words in John 8:32 are echoed by Paul at the start of
Galatians 5. The truth that Jesus gives releases us from bondage.
He releases us from the bondage of our past, of our sins, and of
religion. We are no longer tied to man-made traditions but to the
reality of Christ's kingdom.

Christ has set us free once and for all, and yet we need to
remember this truth throughout our lives. In our humanity,
we are pulled to the regulations of systems and to the promises
of safety within them. Jesus is outside of man-made rules and
governments. His freedom is better than our meager attempts at
control. Let's stand strong in the truth of Christ and remain free
in his love.

*Jesus, I don't want to go back to the bondage that kept me stuck. I
don't want fear to dictate what I will or will not do or be. You are
the final word over my life, and I delight in the freedom you have
given me.*

Love-Filled Faith

When you're joined to the Anointed One, circumcision and religious obligations can benefit you nothing. All that matters now is living in the faith that works and expresses itself through love.

GALATIANS 5:6

The truth that Christ is enough for each of us individually and for us corporately is the truth that Paul is driving home here. Christ is our salvation, the only way to the Father and to complete freedom in his mercy. We are made new not by our rituals and spiritual obligations but through the life of Christ within us through faith.

Christ is our true hope. He has made us right with God. By his Spirit, we eagerly await the return of our Redeemer for the full restoration of all things. Let us continue to run this race of life by faith and in the grace-strength of our Savior. Let us work to express love in all that we do, for true faith is revealed in how we love one another.

Redeemer, thank you for the power of your sacrifice. Thank you for your grace that sets me free to follow in your ways. May my life reflect your powerful mercy as I continually surrender to you and live by faith in your faithfulness.

Called to Freedom

Beloved ones, God has called us to live a life of freedom.
But don't view this wonderful freedom as an excuse
to set up a base of operations in the natural realm.
Constantly love each other and be committed to serve one another.

GALATIANS 5:13

Trrue freedom is found in God's grace, given liberally through Christ. It does not demand perfection. It does not put conditions on us. And yet, we know that we are set free, not so that we can serve ourselves but so that we can serve one another in love.

The love of Christ is liberating. Knowing that he sets us free from sin, not holding any of our mistakes against us, is a wonderfully emancipating reality. When we don't have to hide our hearts from God or others, we are free to live in the full expression of his mercy. We get to choose to partner with God's heart and his kingdom through how we live our lives. What a wonderful opportunity to practice moving in compassion.

Great God, I don't want to build a kingdom for myself on this earth. I want to live out your love that has transformed my heart and life. Show me ways that I can serve others today in your mercy. I use my freedom for your glory.

The Law of Love

For all the law can be summarized in one grand statement:
"Demonstrate love to your neighbor,
even as you care for and love yourself."

GALATIANS 5:14

Our heart attitudes are clear before the Lord. He reads us like an open book, seeing the nuance and source of every thought, feeling, and choice. We partner with Christ when we align our hearts and lives in the law of his love.

When critical attitudes abound, fellowship erodes. Even if we do not express these thoughts to others, the soil of our hearts is affected. The love of Christ compels us toward one another; it does not drive us apart through judgment toward each other. An act of surrendered, fervent love overcomes a multitude of sins, and it has the ability to restore broken trust (1 Peter 4:8). May we be known by our love, not by our biting opinions.

Loving Father, I admit where I have gotten it wrong and become distracted by differing opinions rather than seeing my brothers and sisters through eyes of compassion. Help me to remain rooted in humanity and in your humility as I look for ways to demonstrate love to those around me.

Soaring with the Spirit

> When you yield to the life of the Spirit,
> you will no longer be living under the law,
> but soaring above it!
>
> GALATIANS 5:18

Are you looking for a way to move past the old cycles of cravings that pull you into a place where you feel stuck? Are you longing for a way to rise above the endless and changing requirements of this world? If you yield to the life of the Spirit, you will soar above it. The liberty of Christ lifts you, and the Spirit of God moves you with the wind of his presence.

You can trust the Spirit's leadership, for the Spirit is the breath of God. The Holy Spirit is living and active, moving today. There is unhindered fellowship with God through his Spirit. There is peace, joy, comfort, and hope in his presence. May we not be burdened down by the pull of the cravings of self-life but soar above them in the new creation life of the Spirit within us.

Holy Spirit, I yield my heart and my life to you. I don't want to continue to be pulled into self-defeating cycles. Transform me, lead me, and liberate me in your power.

Spirit Fruit

But the fruit produced by the Holy Spirit within you is divine love in all its varied expressions: joy that overflows, peace that subdues, patience that endures, kindness in action, a life full of virtue, faith that prevails, gentleness of heart, and strength of spirit. Never set the law above these qualities, for they are meant to be limitless.

GALATIANS 5:22–23

Perhaps you find yourself in need of a reminder of what the behavior of self-life looks like in our lives. If that's the case, read Galatians 5:19–21. The fruit of the Spirit, as Paul continues in verses 22 and 23, are in stark contrast, and yet it is what we hear over and over again through the Word.

The harvest of God's work within us is evident in the fruit that our lives bear. Divine love is the ultimate fruit, and all the other virtues mentioned are revelatory aspects of the *agape* of God. The fruit of the Spirit is living and active, not simply ideological virtues. Where there is overflowing joy, subduing peace, enduring patience, active kindness, a virtuous life, prevailing faith, a heart of gentleness, and strength of spirit, there is evidence of the Spirit's work in our lives.

Spirit, I won't put rule-abiding above any virtue of your kingdom. Move in my life, for I am yielded to you.

Gentle Restoration

My beloved friends, if you see a believer who is overtaken with a fault, the one who is in the Spirit should seek to restore him in the Spirit of gentleness. But keep watch over your own heart so that you won't be tempted to exalt yourself over him.

GALATIANS 6:1

The love of God is laced with kindness. It is ripe with gentleness to restore. It does not demure from reality or hard truths, but it also does not seek to shame or demean others. If we cannot feel the gentleness of the Spirit toward the person, also known as compassion, then we should not confront them about their faults until we do.

Pride will not serve us or them. Being overly critical and judgmental of our brothers and sisters while ignoring the planks in our own eyes is not recommended. Jesus warned of this in Matthew 7:5 when he said, "First acknowledge and deal with your own 'blind spots,' and then you'll be capable of dealing with the 'blind spot' of your friend." As in all things, humility coupled with love will never steer us wrong.

Jesus, I'm so grateful for your kindness that leads to repentance. I reject the urge to judge, manipulate, or cut off my friends, and I instead invite your mercy to lead me toward redemptive restoration.

Empowered by Love

Love empowers us to fulfill the law of the Anointed One
as we carry each other's troubles. If you think you are
somebody too important to stoop down to help another
(when really you are not), you are living in deception.

GALATIANS 6:2–3

The way of Christ is not like the ways of this world. His love empowers us to help and support each other in our troubles. Capitalistic societies say that we should think of ourselves as the most important people—our freedoms, our opportunities, and our comfort levels. And yet, in the kingdom of Christ, we are called to serve each other in love. No one is more important or greater than anyone else.

Is this reflected in our personal worldviews? Or are we so conditioned by our culture that we do not take the words of Christ seriously? None of us is too important to take time to stoop to help those who need it. In fact, we are all in need of this kind of loving care and attention. Let's be like living lights of Christ's love in this world.

God of mercy, your love empowers me to see outside of myself. Your love levels the playing field and reaches out to everyone in the same overflowing measure. I humble my heart before you and ask for a greater revelation of your mercy.

Joyful Devotion

Let everyone be devoted to fulfill the work God has given them to do with excellence, and their joy will be in doing what's right and being themselves, and not in being affirmed by others.

GALATIANS 6:4

What a wonderfully liberating exhortation this is. We do not need to "find ourselves" or figure out what grand purpose we serve in the kingdom of God. Our lives matter as much here and now in the mundane aspects of our lives and responsibilities as they ever will—even living out our dreams.

Rather than being overly focused on how we can improve our situations, looking to the future for our purpose and fulfillment, let's look at what is ours right now. Whatever work is ours to do, let's do it with excellence for the Lord. As we do what is right and are completely ourselves instead of trying to be like others, we become free in the joy of God's present favor over us.

Creator, thank you for who you have made me to be. Thank you for who I am right now and for your love, acceptance, and empowerment in the life I am already living. I give you my joyful devotion.

Self-Government

Every believer is ultimately responsible
for his or her own conscience.

GALATIANS 6:5

One of the most liberating realizations that we can have is that we are ultimately responsible for ourselves. We cannot control how others respond, how they will choose to live, or whether they will understand us. But we can, should, and must be the leaders of our own lives. Only we know the inner workings of our minds. We and God.

When we experience the joy of doing what is ours to do, when we choose for ourselves to follow Christ and his kingdom ways in our lives as they are, we take responsibility over our actions. Do we have to work, or do we get to work? Do we have to spend time with our families, or do we get the privilege of being with them? Let's look at our heart attitudes and take joyous responsibility over what is ours.

Jesus, where I have looked at my life and seen only what is lacking, help me to see what I already have and the gifts that my life holds right now. I get to make choices today, and I choose to look through your lens of love. Thank you for the freedom of choice and partnership with you.

Plant Good Seeds

The harvest you reap reveals the seed that you planted. If you plant the corrupt seeds of self-life into this natural realm, you can expect a harvest of corruption. If you plant the good seeds of Spirit-life you will reap beautiful fruits that grow from the everlasting life of the Spirit.

GALATIANS 6:8

The principle of sowing and reaping is as simple as it gets. "What you plant will always be the very thing you harvest" (Galatians 6:7). We shouldn't be startled that if we sow seeds of bitterness, then we reap offense and hatred. Nor should we be surprised at harvesting peace in our relationships when we sow loyalty, respect, and honesty.

Seasons of sowing will not always be pleasant. As we plant seeds in the soil of grief, it will be painful. God is not outside of this process. He is in it with us. As we yield to his Spirit, he waters the seeds of new life with our tears. We can only do our part and ask God to bless it. Let's keep choosing the Spirit-life whenever we think of it, and may our hearts remain surrendered to his mercy in all things.

Holy Spirit, I'm grateful for the awareness that I can choose what seeds I will sow, and at the same time, your mercy covers my mistakes and missteps when I submit them to you.

Keep Sowing

Don't allow yourselves to be weary in planting good seeds, for the season of reaping the wonderful harvest you've planted is coming!

GALATIANS 6:9

A re you weary of hard days running into each other? Have you grown tired of doing the right thing? We all grow weak in this world, but the Spirit of God offers grace to fill us up with his strength any time we need it. Paul echoes his sentiment in this verse elsewhere, when he says, "Brothers and sisters, don't ever grow weary in doing what is right" (2 Thessalonians 3:13).

When we work as worship, sowing seeds of his kingdom values into the soil of our lives, we will reap a harvest when the time is right. Let us be cognizant of the season that we are in. What if a farmer simply got tired of planting his seeds and gave up? When the harvest time rolled around, he would regret his decision. Let's be like wise and steadfast farmers, doing what is ours to do with the foresight to know that it will be worth it when harvest time comes.

Father, I will not give up planting good seeds. I partner with your mercy, and I ask for your grace-strength to empower me in endurance. I believe it will be worth it.

Seize Today's Opportunities

Take advantage of every opportunity to be a blessing to others, especially to our brothers and sisters in the family of faith!

GALATIANS 6:10

E very day affords us opportunities to partner with the Lord's love in blessing others. What extra effort would it take for us to look for ways to encourage others in practical acts today? Perhaps we could buy someone a meal, offer a ride to a neighbor who has trouble getting around, take the time to encourage a friend with a gift card to a favorite place. The possibilities are endless.

Ask the Holy Spirit to inspire you and open your eyes to opportunities at your fingertips. A little sacrifice of time, money, or something else that's valuable to you may do a lot to buoy someone else's hope. It will also encourage your own heart as you partner with the Lord in his unconditional love.

Faithful One, open my eyes to see where I could partner with your grace to offer someone else a helping hand. Give me ears to hear the Spirit's leadership. I am yours, and I choose to partner with you.

Lavished in Love

Every spiritual blessing in the heavenly realm has already been lavished upon us as a love gift from our wonderful heavenly Father, the Father of our Lord Jesus—all because he sees us wrapped into Christ. This is why we celebrate him with all our hearts!

EPHESIANS 1:3

As devoted believers, we are wrapped up in Christ and have been made holy by being united with him. He lavished his love upon us, and we have every spiritual blessing available through fellowship with him. His generous grace is our endless portion.

As we focus on the gift of communion with Christ through his Spirit that dwells within us, let's give him our attention. May the prayers of our hearts be like incense that effortlessly releases its fragrance in the atmosphere of his presence. With open hearts to receive his overwhelming mercy, let's release the worship of our love to him.

Lord Jesus, I celebrate your incomparable love with the awe of a dearly loved child who has caught a glimpse of the glory of your goodness. Thank you for the spiritual blessings I continually discover in your mercy.

August

Chosen

In love he chose us before he laid
the foundation of the universe!

EPHESIANS 1:4

B efore God even formed the foundation of the earth, he chose
to bestow upon us his affection. He held nothing back in
love then, and he doesn't hold back his mercy from us now. If
we are in Christ, we are new creations, innocent and pure before
him. We are chosen children, never to be abandoned or rejected
by him.

Everything God does, he does in love. The very essence of
his being is love. When we become more like him, we live out his
compassionate mercy. We offer kindness and gentleness. We tell
the truth without demeaning those who disagree. We live with
integrity, knowing it is better to be free in the liberty of God's
love than to be bound to the empty promises of self-promotion.
As the psalmist famously penned, "Just one day of intimacy with
you is like a thousand days of joy rolled into one!" (Psalm 84:10).
We have been chosen to know him intimately even as we are fully
known by him.

*Wonderful One, there is no one else like you on all the earth. I am
grateful to be known by you, and I long to know you more intimately.*

Waterfalls of Grace

Since we are now joined to Christ, we have been given the treasures of redemption by his blood—the total cancellation of our sins—all because of the cascading riches of his grace.

EPHESIANS 1:7

There is tremendous relief in forgiveness. When we humble ourselves in repentance, and we are offered understanding and exoneration, there is little else that can compare to the profound gratitude we feel in response. In Christ, we have been fully forgiven of our sins. Even what others cannot release us from, he does not hold against us.

How, then, will we exemplify the cascading riches of God's grace in our own relationships? How does redemption have a place in our earthly communities? We should never use God's mercy as a weapon against those who have been victimized. We can only choose forgiveness for ourselves, not force others into what they are not ready to do. Let's look at our own hearts, our own relationships, and our own part. That is always the place to start.

Gracious Father, thank you for the cascading riches of your grace. Thank you for canceling the debt of my sins with the redemption power of your blood. May my heart become more like yours as I release the need for revenge.

Illuminated and Inspired

I pray that the light of God will illuminate the eyes of your imagination, flooding you with light, until you experience the full revelation of the hope of his calling—that is, the wealth of God's glorious inheritances that he finds in us, his holy ones.

EPHESIANS 1:18

The light of God illuminates our understanding with revelation knowledge. It floods us with light, until we see the clear picture of what we've been called into. As long as it is called today, there is more to discover in Christ. There is more to uncover in his glorious love.

In the light of Christ, we can see ourselves more clearly. The light of his mercy shines and burns off the fog of our muddied minds. The world is constantly telling us to do more. Everyone has a different opinion about what will work to get us to our goals. And yet, the values of the kingdom are guideposts not hard-and-fast rules to follow to help us discern the hope of our calling as followers of Jesus. Let's look for our inspiration in the one who created it all.

Masterful Creator, there is nothing that you cannot do, and there is no path unknown to you. I follow your leadership, and I lean on your wisdom to illuminate my understanding.

Look to Him

He alone is the leader and source of everything needed in the church. God has put everything beneath the authority of Jesus Christ and has given him the highest rank above all others.

EPHESIANS 1:22

When we look to others to fix our problems before we look to the Lord for his living wisdom, we reveal where our true trust lies. Jesus Christ is not only the head and leader of the church, but he is also the source of everything we need. No pastor is above him, no matter how charismatic they may seem. Jesus is the final authority always.

Let's hold everything up to the light of Christ. The wisdom of God is purer than the opinions of powerful men. His leadership is full of loyal love and mighty mercy. He alone is our judge, so let's stop judging each other so harshly. His kindness, and not how right he is, leads us to repentance even though his truth is unmarred by man's estimations. In all things, let's look to Christ. He is our leader, our Savior, and our ultimate example.

Jesus Christ, your ways are unparalleled. You don't seek to control us or keep us under your thumb but to set us free from our sin. Thank you for the wisdom of your ways. You are the ultimate example and the one I look to in all things.

Lush with Mercy

God still loved us with such great love.
He is so rich in compassion and mercy.

EPHESIANS 2:4

How wonderful it is that we are set free from living the self-life that Paul describes. Instead of living "by whatever natural cravings and thoughts our minds dictated" (Ephesians 2:3), we have the Spirit to empower us with peace, a sound mind, and self-control. And it is all fueled by the compassion and mercy of our loving Jesus.

Even when we were lost in our own destructive patterns, God loved us more than we can imagine. His love for us has not grown since we yielded our lives to him—it's just that we are awakened to it. And what a glorious love it is. May we choose to follow Christ every step of the way. He is trustworthy and faithful, and his character will never change.

Great God, your mercy-kindness draws me to you again and again. It is astounding that we could never overestimate or exaggerate it. Thank you for your incomparably glorious and endlessly liberating love.

Seated with Christ

He raised us up with Christ the exalted One, and we ascended with him into the glorious perfection and authority of the heavenly realm, for we are now co-seated as one with Christ!

EPHESIANS 2:6

What a glorious mystery it is that we can be seated in heavenly places with Christ even before we see him face-to-face. Our identities have already been stamped with the approval of God in Christ. We are under his covering of purity and mercy, and his perfection and authority are like a canopy over us.

Even when we are weak, we are completely and fully accepted in the love of Christ. When we mess up and fail, Christ's mercy meets us. We are never without it. Let's look to him for our approval, for his opinion of us and his declaration over us are what truly matter. We have already been raised up into our glorious perfection even as we wade through the muddy waters of this world.

Lord Jesus, I lay down before you the areas that I am struggling with, and I ask you to give me your higher perspective. Let me see from your vantage point, where I have already been raised to life in you. Thank you.

Poetic Expressions

We have become his poetry, a re-created people that will fulfill the destiny he has given each of us, for we are joined to Jesus, the Anointed One. Even before we were born, God planned in advance our destiny and the good works we would do to fulfill it!

EPHESIANS 2:10

Our yielded lives are beautiful, poetic expressions written by God. Everyone is unique and beautiful. His creativity shines through us, and what a glorious identity it is to be known as a piece of his artistry. May we look through our lives with this lens today, as we consider that we are valuable originals, none of us a print of someone else.

How does the creativity of your Maker shine through your unique experience? What makes you *you*? Instead of comparing yourself to others today, rejoice in the beauty that is yours and no one else's. Celebrate the unique voice, style, talent, or perspective that you have to offer this world. You are a living reflection of his love.

Creator, I believe that I am made in your image, a unique expression of your creative hand. Speak your words of life over me today and encourage my heart in your perspective of who I am.

Prince of Peace

Our reconciling "Peace" is Jesus! He has made Jew and non-Jew one in Christ. By dying as our sacrifice, he has broken down every wall of prejudice that separated us and has now made us equal through our union with Christ.

EPHESIANS 2:14

There is no excuse for harboring prejudices against one another based on a false hierarchy. In Christ, we are one; we are equal. Jesus Christ is the Prince of Peace, and he is our reconciler before the Father. He is the head of the church, and we are his body. No part is better than another, no matter how prominent we may or may not be.

Where are the dividing lines of injustice hiding within the bounds of our families, communities, and churches? Where are we looking to hide behind walls that Jesus already broke down in his mercy? Let's stop assembling bricks of hostility and instead reach out in compassion to one another.

Peace Giver, you are constantly reaching out in loyal love to us, and I open my heart to receive a fresh portion of your clarifying mercy. Move my heart in your love and reframe my vision in your truth.

Beyond Understanding

Grace alone empowers me so that I can boldly preach
this wonderful message to non-Jewish people,
sharing with them the unfading, inexhaustible riches of Christ,
which are beyond comprehension.

EPHESIANS 3:8

Grace was what empowered Paul in his ministry, and it is the power of God's Spirit with us today. Whatever we need, there is grace for in Christ. We can only get so far in our own abilities. God's grace empowers us in our weakness, and it yields fruit far better than we could cultivate without him.

The riches of Christ are inexhaustible. There is no end to the benefit of knowing him. May we press further into his heart through the presence of his Spirit today. Let's dive deep into the wisdom of his perspective and break out of the smallness of our own thinking. He invites us, with open arms of mercy, into the great expanse of his kingdom. Let's look to him for our daily bread and seek his face with all our energy.

Jesus, thank you for not despising my weakness. I come to you with the reality of my experience right here and now, and I don't hold back from you. Transform my perspective in the grand and clarifying wisdom of your own.

Royal Welcome

This perfectly wise plan was destined from eternal ages and fulfilled completely in our Lord Jesus Christ, so that now we have boldness through him, and free access as kings before the Father because of our complete confidence in Christ's faithfulness.

EPHESIANS 3:11–12

There is a difference between pride and confidence. Pride says that I am better than others. Confidence says that I know who I am, and I am unashamed of my identity. Pride uses comparison to lift oneself up by demeaning others. Confidence does not compete for attention because its strength flows from within.

As children of God, we can come to him with complete confidence in his love over us because of Christ. Christ's faithfulness does not depend on our faith, and yet we have the opportunity to increase our confidence as we put our trust in him. We are welcomed as kings and queens, with full access to our glorious Father and the King of kings. Let us throw off everything that hinders us in love and come freely to him today.

Jesus, you are my confidence and strength. I don't need to measure my life next to anyone but to you, and you say that I am wholly loved and accepted. Thank you.

Flooded by Love

I pray that he would unveil within you the unlimited riches of his glory and favor until supernatural strength floods your innermost being with his divine might and explosive power.

EPHESIANS 3:16

Are you in need of supernatural strength today? Are you limited in your resources of love, patience, peace, and joy? Has your hope dwindled with the weariness of living in this world? If you are tuned in to a longing or lack within your heart, soul, or body, turn to the Lord and the fullness of his presence with you now.

Invite God's love to overflow you, to flood you with its supernatural strength. Receive the divine might and explosive power of Christ's resurrection life within your innermost being. The Spirit of God is not stingy, and he does not dole his grace out in metered measure. He is an overflowing fountain, a rushing river, and a gushing waterfall of all that you need. He is the purest source, and he is full of everything you long for.

Mighty God, I know that all my longings find their ultimate fulfillment in you. You are the perfect Father, the most loyal lover, the closest friend, and the most powerful and merciful leader. Fill me up with your living love yet again.

Endless, Extravagant Love

The astonishing love of Christ in all its dimensions. How deeply intimate and far-reaching is his love! How enduring and inclusive it is! Endless love beyond measurement that transcends our understanding—this extravagant love pours into you until you are filled to overflowing with the fullness of God!

EPHESIANS 3:18–19

The unparalleled love of God cannot be exaggerated. In fact, if it doesn't sound too good to be true, then we are settling for far less than it actually is. The Word of God says that his love transcends our understanding. Even if we try to grasp its magnitude, we fall short. And yet, what a worthy pursuit!

The love of Christ is extravagant. When we partner our faith with his faithfulness, our hearts become resting places of his love. His love becomes the source and root of our very lives (Ephesians 3:17). May we continue to press in to the presence of God with faith, growing in knowledge of who he is and being constantly transformed into his image. There is always more to discover, more to experience, and more to behold in him.

Lord, I cannot begin to understand your love, but it leaves me in awe every time a catch a new glimpse of what your glorious mercy is like. Open my eyes in a new way today.

Choose Trust

> Never doubt God's mighty power to work in you and accomplish all this. He will achieve infinitely more than your greatest request, your most unbelievable dream, and exceed your wildest imagination! He will outdo them all, for his miraculous power constantly energizes you.
>
> EPHESIANS 3:20

Jesus is trustworthy. His love for you burns more brightly than you know. It is fierce and pure. He loves you with limitless love. He extends kindness after kindness toward you. He is able to do far more than you can imagine ever asking him to do. Will you raise your faith to the level of God's faithfulness? Will you trust him to fill the gaps of your understanding and meet you where you need him to?

Imagine your most unbelievable dream. Now consider God, in his goodness, can do even better than that. God is not a magician who magically answers your prayers as you expect him to. He sees things that you cannot perceive, and he is more creative than you can imagine. Trust him. Above all, fill up on the fellowship of his Spirit. There is courage, strength, hope, and peace in him. In the waiting, press into the fullness of his truth.

Spirit, you overwhelm my meager ideas of goodness with the faithfulness of your loving-kindness. What you do is better than I could ask for. I trust you.

No Excuses

With tender humility and quiet patience, always demonstrate
gentleness and generous love toward one another,
especially toward those who may try your patience.

EPHESIANS 4:2

In Christ, there is no excuse for our bad behavior. We should
not look for ways to escape accountability. If the loyal love of
God fills us and leads us, then we will be known by our humility. We will choose restoration and reconciliation over being
right. We will extend kindness and patience rather than lose our
tempers. And even when we get it wrong, we will seek forgiveness
from those we hurt.

When we look at our lives, where do we see *tender humility*
and *quiet patience* on display? Where is *gentleness* and *generous
love* abounding? May we take hold of every opportunity to practice choosing these things instead of our own comfort. May we
look for ways to lift others up—to build them up in love—instead
of ways to cut them down to size. Let's be living reflections of
Christ's love in this world.

*Jesus, I want to reflect your kindness, gentleness, patience, and
humility in my relationships. I see where I can fall short, but you
empower me in your love to choose humble kindness. I want to be
like you.*

Sweet Harmony

For the Lord God is one, and so are we,
for we share in one faith, one baptism, and one Father.

EPHESIANS 4:5

In verse 3 of this chapter Paul says, "Be faithful to guard the sweet harmony of the Holy Spirit among you in the bonds of peace." In Christ, we are one with all other believers. We are part of one family and of one body over which Christ is the head. Where we have many denominations and sects of Christianity, Christ does not separate. This means that we are brothers and sisters in the faith with *all* who believe Christ is the Son of God and have yielded their lives to him.

With this in mind, how can we promote the peace of God that we find in his Spirit? How can we guard the harmony of his love in our relationships and communities? In Christ, we have more that unites us than separates us: namely, love. Let's choose that love in our hearts first and then as an overflow into every part of our lives.

Father, thank you for the unity we find in your Spirit through your Son. Release a greater passion for true peace and harmony that does not shy away from hard truths. I believe your ways are better than our own. I choose to follow your example.

Abundant Grace

He has generously given each one of us supernatural grace,
according to the size of the gift of Christ.

EPHESIANS 4:7

No one is excluded from the wonderfully abundant grace of God in Christ. We all come to him with hearts open to receive, and he meets us with his generously overflowing measure. We each have different needs, but his grace is the same grace poured out on each one. The size of what we receive is not dependent on us but on Christ. So, then, let's rejoice in the abundance that is ours in him.

If we struggle to see how God's supernatural grace meets us, let's ask God for revelation. Let's look to him for understanding. None of us who choose Christ are without the grace of his presence, so let's lean on him for the help we need to comprehend. He is so very good, and he will not fail us.

Gracious God, thank you for the supernatural strength of your Spirit. I need you today to enlighten the eyes of my heart and open my understanding to who you are in Spirit and in truth. Help me to recognize your abundant grace.

Appointed

He has appointed some with grace to be apostles, and some with grace to be prophets, and some with grace to be evangelists, and some with grace to be pastors, and some with grace to be teachers.

EPHESIANS 4:11

Paul lays out the appointed gifts within the ministry model of the church in this passage. Some are called as apostles, some as prophets, and some as evangelists. Some are appointed as pastors and some as teachers. Paul describes these gifts as "grace ministries" (v. 13). They are for the building up and nurturing of believers.

Every calling to ministry is done by the grace of God, and it is followed out with grace as well. Christ leads us, and all our direction and ministry flows from his guidance. The one who preaches is not more important than the one who serves behind the scenes, for it is all for the building up of the body of Christ. May we recognize and honor the gracious gift of calling over our lives, and may we encourage one another in these gifts as long as it is today.

Lord Jesus, thank you for your leadership over my life and over your church. I join with your heart and am empowered by your grace-strength to follow through on what you call me to. I follow your lead.

Recreated in Righteousness

Now it's time to be made new by every revelation that's been given to you. And to be transformed as you embrace the glorious Christ-within as your new life and live in union with him! For God has re-created you all over again in his perfect righteousness, and you now belong to him in the realm of true holiness.

EPHESIANS 4:23–24

Now is the time to allow the revelation of Christ to transform our minds. We are made new in the powerful presence of Jesus, and every new glimpse of his incomparable wisdom is an opportunity to change. As we embrace the glorious Spirit of Christ within us, we become more like him.

How can you embrace his Spirit in you today? What can you do to turn your attention toward him more often throughout your day? The Father does not hold your past against you, for he finds you pure in the mercy-covering of Christ over your life. Walk in the freedom of his love. Live out his kindness as you receive expanded understanding of his incomparable power.

Jesus, you are my covering, and you make me holy. I give up trying to prove myself to you and others and instead choose to live out of the overflowing mercy you offer. Thank you for making me new and removing my shame.

Living Reflections

Be imitators of God in everything you do,
for then you will represent your Father
as his beloved sons and daughters.

EPHESIANS 5:1

God's desire is that we be like him and be filled with all that he is. As we perceive his thoughts, we can see from his perspective. As we fill up on his love, we have a well of kindness and compassion to offer others. When we become like God in our choices and actions, we reflect his likeness in our lives. When we meditate on his character, we learn to value what he values.

God is like the sun, and we are like stars reflecting his light. We don't need to produce our own light; rather, we shine because the brightness of the Son reaches out toward us. The more we turn to him, the brighter we sparkle. The more we look to him in all that we do, the more we receive from the outpouring of his glory. He is our source.

Bright Morning Star, I want to reflect your likeness in my life. As I turn to you, reveal the glory of your character more and more. I want to be filled with your love, joy, peace, patience, kindness, and justice. Shine bright from my life.

What Goodness

The supernatural fruits of his light will be seen in you—
goodness, righteousness, and truth.

EPHESIANS 5:9

When we are unified with the Lord Jesus, we have the very light of God shining through us. Our lives become reflections of his kingdom. Goodness, righteousness, and truth shine like beacons from the revelation-light we receive directly from his Spirit.

When we make it our mission to live as vessels flooded with the revelation of God, our own opinions become less important in the perspective of God's values. We learn to lead with mercy instead of judgment. We stand on truth, not letting the winds of the world's whims blow us to and fro. His loving-kindness is our foundation, and we build our lives upon his faithfulness.

Faithful One, you are the goodness that shines from my life. As I look to you today, flood my mind and heart with your revelation-light. Pour out of my life with the gracious overflow of your mercy that constantly rains over me.

Life-Giving Light

Whatever the revelation-light exposes, it will also correct,
and everything that reveals truth is light to the soul.

EPHESIANS 5:13

Are there any areas of your life that remain hidden? There is no need to keep anything from God. His light shines on our hearts and reveals everything that is there. He does not deal in shame or control us with condescension. He is infinitely kind, irrepressibly merciful, and he reconciles what we cannot make right on our own.

Will you invite the Spirit to shine his light on your inner world? What is exposed in the truth of his light, he will also correct. When he corrects, he does so in love. May you rejoice in the truth that sets you free. May you find your spirits lifted as you are fully embraced by the love of your Father. Let him correct what needs to be corrected and let him speak life to your weary heart. He will love you to life in the warmth of his presence.

Holy One, I trust you to reveal with your revelation-light what needs to be exposed within me. I trust your loving-kindness to draw me toward you as you restore what needs to be rebuilt in your mercy.

Living Honorably

Be very careful how you live, not being like those with no
understanding, but live honorably with true wisdom,
for we are living in evil times. Take full advantage of every day
as you spend your life for his purposes.

EPHESIANS 5:15–16

As the days run into each other, we can get so caught up in
the busyness of our lives and responsibilities that we forget
to pay attention to our values. There will always be more to do
if we look at life as an endless checklist. However, all we have is
this moment. Do we leave time to rest and recharge? Do we make
space for loved ones and community care?

True wisdom does not rush from one obligation to the next.
It knows what is most important and makes room. True wisdom
realizes that becoming more present in our lives means tuning
into our values and making changes to live according to them.
Honorable living is intentional; it does not happen by chance.
May we live into this awareness, turning our attention to the Lord
and to what we know is our part in the here and now.

*Wise God, there is no other God before or after you. All wisdom is
from you and found in you. I look to you even as I become more
aware of the gift of the present moment.*

All the Time

> Always do what is right and not only when others are watching,
> so that you may please Christ as his servants by doing his will.
>
> EPHESIANS 6:6

Integrity keeps us doing what is right at all times whether or not anyone else will ever acknowledge or see it. Honesty keeps us accountable before the Lord, and humility keeps us relying on the Spirit's grace to empower us in self-control.

May we be people of our word, following through on what we say we will do. May we be honest and steadfast, showing up when it matters. May we be faithful in the little things as well as the big things in life. Let's remember to continually live with the values of Christ's kingdom in full view, guiding us each and every day. God sees it all. When we do the right thing, we need never worry being "found out."

Steadfast One, may your unchanging values guide me in my choices all the days of my life. Let the grace of your presence empower me to choose your ways over the easy outs every single time.

The Excellent Way

Be assured that anything you do that is beautiful and excellent will be repaid by our Lord, whether you are an employee or an employer.

EPHESIANS 6:8

When we do anything, may we be reminded that it is not meaningless. Whatever we do, when we do it from a place of integrity and unto the Lord, it is an act of worship. When we choose the excellent way instead of the easy way out, we honor the Lord with our actions. When we commit to the right way, we distinguish ourselves in his eyes.

When it is a sacrifice to choose compassion over self-preservation, let's remember that the Spirit of God is our strength and our support. His presence is with us, and he honors every move we make in mercy. Let's give ourselves to choosing the beautiful and excellent things, no matter our station or responsibilities. God is faithful, and he will meet us in every movement of surrender.

Beautiful Lord, I cannot help but be captured by your mercy-kindness. Your ways are unlike the ways of the power hungry. Fill me with your Spirit and lead me in your love. I choose to walk in your beautiful footsteps.

Victorious Strength

Now my beloved ones, I have saved these most important truths for last: Be supernaturally infused with strength through your life-union with the Lord Jesus. Stand victorious with the force of his explosive power flowing in and through you.

EPHESIANS 6:10

Life in Christ is not passive. Life, in general, is a mix of what happens to us and what we choose. We cannot control how the future will turn out, but we can choose how we will respond and act in every moment. Instead of getting stuck in the overwhelming center of what-ifs, let's remain rooted in the reality of what is ours to do in the here and now.

There is supernatural strength available from the living communion we have with the Spirit of God. We have been joined to the Lord Jesus heart-to-heart, and his powerful resurrection life transforms us from the inside out. Today, let's stand in the victory of God's explosive power that flows in and through us.

Holy Spirit, fill me to overflow with the fiery power of your love. Your grace-strength becomes the well from which I draw. Thank you for this day that I can choose to walk in the ways of your kingdom.

Always Pray

Pray passionately in the Spirit,
as you constantly intercede
with every form of prayer at all times.
Pray the blessings of God upon all his believers.

EPHESIANS 6:18

With our hearts yielded to God and our lives open to him, we become living prayers before God. We can keep a consistently open line of communication between us and the throne of God. He hears our cries, notices our leanings, and reads the longings of our hearts.

Why would we withhold prayer when God is our ever-present help in times of trouble? Why would we keep ourselves from opening up to him when he shares in our joys and victories? We also get to share in his. Let's lean into the presence of God, for he is steadfast and good. He is loving and true. He is loyal and kind. He is strong and wise. He never turns us away when we turn to him.

Jesus, you are my prayer partner in all things. I want to develop such an openhearted relationship with you that it is an ongoing, continuous conversation between you and me. I will offer up my prayers continually, and I know that you will lead me, answer me, and keep me, just as you will with all who call on your name.

Fully Convinced

I pray with great faith for you, because I'm fully convinced that the One who began this gracious work in you will faithfully continue the process of maturing you until the unveiling of our Lord Jesus Christ!

PHILIPPIANS 1:6

Where does our faith stem from? Is it from the experience of others alone, the testimonies of God's goodness being worked out throughout history? These are stepping-stones that we can walk along, and yet, the substance of our faith is from the source of everything. Our faith comes from the Creator.

Hebrews 11:1 states, "Faith brings our hopes into reality and becomes the foundation needed to acquire the things we long for. It is all the evidence required to prove what is still unseen." When we pray, let's do it from a place of conviction that flows from the faithful love of God within us. What God has begun, he will faithfully continue. He is not finished with us yet.

Faithful One, thank you for the faith you have planted in my heart. May it expand in the water of your faithful mercy, expanding as it grows under the love-light of your presence. Increase my faith as I continue to look to your faithfulness. Encourage my heart in your tangible goodness.

Keep Increasing

I continue to pray for your love to grow and increase beyond measure, bringing you into the rich revelation of spiritual insight in all things.

PHILIPPIANS 1:9

In Christ, we are living reflections of his love in this world. There is always more to learn of his kingdom, more love to experience, and more joy to take hold of. His marvelous grace is abundantly more than we could ever imagine. We cannot over-state the magnitude of his wonderful mercy in our lives. Just as the kingdom of God is ever increasing, so can our knowledge, our experience, and our hope.

Paul says in 2 Corinthians 3:18 that "we can all draw close to him with the veil removed from our faces. And with no veil we all become like mirrors who brightly reflect the glory of the Lord Jesus…we move from one brighter level of glory to another." We are going from one level of glory to another. Today is yet another opportunity to move closer to Christ and experience new measures of his wonderful love that brings revelation, confidence, and clarity.

Lord Jesus, truly there is no one better than you. Though I have known goodness in my relationships, your love is even purer, brighter, and always life-giving. Continue to expand my understanding in your limitless mercy.

Continue to Cling

> No matter what, I will continue to hope and passionately
> cling to Christ, so that he will be openly revealed through me
> before everyone's eyes. So I will not be ashamed!
> In my life or in my death, Christ will be magnified in me.
>
> PHILIPPIANS 1:20

P aul wrote these words from a prison cell. He was not so discouraged from his circumstances that he lost sight of God's faithful power. He was not overcome with dejection in his circumstances that he failed to believe that God could work in wonderfully miraculous ways, no matter whether he lived or died. Paul's preoccupation was not with his physical deliverance but in the growth of the pure and simple gospel through the message of his life.

Paul's encouragement to the believers in Philippi is an important message for us today. No matter what, let's continue to hope and passionately cling to Christ. Let's let joy overflow from our hearts as we continue to stand on the foundation of the mercy of Christ in our lives. His faithfulness is sure, and he will not give up on his mission to powerfully transform and save all who come to him.

Messiah, I choose to cling to hope in your faithfulness and passionately hold onto your powerful truth. You are better than my circumstances, and I believe that you will not let me go.

Grounded in the Gospel

Whatever happens, keep living your lives based on the reality of the gospel of Christ. Then when I come to see you, or hear good reports of you, I'll know that you stand united in one Spirit and one passion.

PHILIPPIANS 1:27

Today is the perfect opportunity to take a moment and evaluate our hearts, our focus, and our lives around the gospel of Christ. What are we basing our decisions on? How are we evaluating our choices? As Paul stated, "Whatever happens, keep living your lives based on the reality of the gospel of Christ."

When life is going well, without the upset of unexpected trials, our hearts may feel at rest and content. But what of storms and troubles, disheartening diagnoses, and sudden losses? Do we lose our peace and question God's faithfulness? The reality of the gospel of Christ is steadfast and firm, no matter our circumstances. Even as we suffer, we are called to endure conflict without giving up hope, for God's mercy is relentless and is working even then.

Redeemer, I know that you are a master restorer and that when you promise something, you are loyal to your Word. I trust that when you said you would never leave or abandon your people, that you meant it, and I am included in that.

Love that Comforts

Look at how much encouragement you've found in your relationship with the Anointed One! You are filled to overflowing with his comforting love. You have experienced a deepening friendship with the Holy Spirit and have felt his tender affection and mercy.

PHILIPPIANS 2:1

The love of God is present, and it is comforting. Even in our doubt, when we turn our attention to God in prayer, he breathes peace and encouragement into our hearts with the breath of his Spirit. If you find yourself wanting today, look to him. You don't have to settle for anything less than the overflowing relief and comfort of his powerful love.

The Holy Spirit's friendship is better than anyone can describe with words. The Spirit can minister to deep places within us that no one else can even perceive. May we be encouraged to go to him more and more. As King David proclaimed in Psalm 94:19, "Whenever my busy thoughts were out of control, the soothing comfort of your presence calmed me down and over-whelmed me with delight." May we be met with comfort and joy.

Holy Spirit, move in my heart as I look to you for help. Soothe my worried heart and overwhelm me with delight. Comfort and encourage me. Thank you.

September

Peace and Harmony

I'm asking you, my friends, that you be joined together in perfect unity—
with one heart, one passion, and united in one love. Walk together with
one harmonious purpose and you will fill my heart with unbounded joy.

PHILIPPIANS 2:2

Arguing over our differences will never get us closer to the love and unity of Christ. Every issue that distracts from the love and mercy of Jesus is a secondary one. Let us throw off the things that hinder compassion and kindness and instead look to Jesus as our unifier. When we are united under a shared goal, we will be able to work together with one heart and passion. Forgiveness and restoration will abound. Truth and love will work hand in hand.

Consider the spiritual community that you are a part of. Is it harmonious? What shared vision propels the community in love and care for one another? We each have our part to play in promoting peace and showing the love of Christ in tender acts of mercy toward one another as well as in our larger lives.

Jesus Christ, you are the vision of the church. You are the head. May your name be glorified in our homes, churches, and communities. May your gospel go forth in the purity of your message. Be our peace.

Lamb of God

He humbled himself and became vulnerable, choosing to be revealed as a man and was obedient. He was a perfect example, even in his death—a criminal's death by crucifixion!

PHILIPPIANS 2:8

Jesus did not exploit his divinity as an excuse to stay in heaven, detached from humanity. He laid down his glory in order to take on flesh and bones and to become like us. In his humanity, he humbled himself in vulnerability, choosing to walk in the dust of the earth. All he did, he did in laid-down-love, with our fates in mind.

Christ is our liberating victor. He paved the way to the Father and revealed what God is truly like—merciful beyond measure. Gracious beyond understanding. What a beautiful Savior Christ Jesus is. There is no one else like him. He did not use his power and glory to intimidate or control us. He set it aside so that we might see ourselves in him. He related to us in a way we could understand, so that we might experience the all-surpassing wonders of his grave-robbing power in our lives.

Son of God, thank you for your humility and grace. Thank you for the power of your love. Thank you for your example, and for your fellowship. I cannot fully express the gratitude of my heart, but I will keep thanking you anyway.

Everyone, Everywhere

The authority of the name of Jesus causes every knee to bow in reverence! Everything and everyone will one day submit to this name—in the heavenly realm, in the earthly realm, and in the demonic realm.

PHILIPPIANS 2:10

No one will escape recognizing Jesus' power. Someday, every knee will bow in reverence and honor. One day, every tongue will submit to his holy name, declaring that he is Lord over all and worthy of our praise. Jesus said that if his "followers were silenced, the very stones would break forth with praises!" (Luke 19:40).

May we take this opportunity to align our hearts, minds, and lives in the kingdom of Christ here and now. Why wait until some far-off day to understand that Christ is Lord and full of glory beyond our imagining when we can know and worship him in spirit and truth today?

Lord Jesus, everyone will come under your authority when you return to set every wrong thing right. I choose to live under your lordship now. I bow before you, full of reverence and awe. Lead me in your love and liberate me in your mercy. I won't stop singing your praises, for I believe that you are better than we've yet known.

SEPTEMBER 4

Keep Going

My beloved ones, just like you've always listened to everything I've taught you in the past, I'm asking you now to keep following my instructions as though I were right there with you. Now you must continue to make this new life fully manifested as you live in the holy awe of God—which brings you trembling into his presence.

PHILIPPIANS 2:12

Weariness will, at times, roll in through the cracks of our lives. We will grow tired, so let's prioritize rhythms of rest and renewal. We will get discouraged by the world, so let's dig deep into the loyal love of God that always overflows. Let's be people of perseverance, continuing to push through the service of our lives with integrity and soft hearts.

The value system of the kingdom of Christ never changes. When we align our choices with the priorities of God, there is no need for regret later in life. Wherever this finds you today, keep going. Keep pressing in to know God more through fellowship with his Spirit, filling up on his Word, and encouraging one another in community.

Unfailing One, your grace gives me strength to keep following you on your path of love. Your wisdom brings clarity, and it shows me how to proceed. I trust you, Lord.

Unlimited Joy

My beloved ones, don't ever limit your joy or fail to rejoice
in the wonderful experience of knowing our Lord Jesus!

PHILIPPIANS 3:1

When was the last time you experienced the delicious delight and pure joy of knowing Jesus? There is always a reason to praise him. In his love, he has given you freedom from sin, shame, and fear. His mercy pours over you every day, and it rises to meet you every morning.

There is more relief for your worries, more comfort for your sorrows, and more fulfillment in his care than you have yet realized. You cannot deplete the resources of Christ or his kingdom. What practices of joy can you incorporate in your day? How can you acknowledge the light of his mercy in your life? Look to the little and big miracles of kindness around you. There is always a reason to rejoice.

Joyful Jesus, I want to know the delight of your presence in deeper ways today. Meet me with the wealth of your mercy and overwhelm my heart with your perfect peace and limitless joy. I choose to rejoice in you, Jesus.

Free to Worship

For we have already experienced "heart-circumcision," and we worship God in the power and freedom of the Holy Spirit, not in laws and religious duties. We are those who boast in what Jesus Christ has done, and not in what we can accomplish in our own strength.

PHILIPPIANS 3:3

We cannot make ourselves more acceptable to God through religious rites. Jesus Christ is our covering, our salvation, and our redemption. Through faith in him and through his glorious grace at work within us, we have been saved. We don't please God by cutting things out of our lives. We please him by being united to him through Christ. We then have the liberty to choose how we will express ourselves in him.

The Holy Spirit is the source of power and freedom in worship. In worship, we turn our hearts to God—whether it be alone or with others. The power and freedom of the Holy Spirit rises up within us as we do. Let's measure our lives by the power of God's mercy at work within us, not by the accomplishments of our own hands.

Mighty God, thank you for accepting me as I am, just as I am, whenever I come to you. Your mercy transforms me from the inside out, and your liberating love frees me in authenticity. I worship you.

Incomparable Delight

All of the accomplishments that I once took credit for,
I've now forsaken them and I regard it all as nothing
compared to the delight of experiencing Jesus Christ as my Lord!

PHILIPPIANS 3:7

P aul expands on the sentiment in this verse, continuing, "to truly know him meant letting go of everything from my past and throwing all my boasting on the garbage heap. It's all like a pile of manure to me now" (verse 8). Paul's life before Christ was not insignificant. He had zeal and purpose, power and prestige within the Orthodox Judaic community. And yet, he counts it all as garbage compared to what he has found in Christ.

How has Christ revolutionized your life? What beauty has come from his mercy at work within you? How has following Jesus affected the quality of your life? May you find overwhelming delight in his presence today. May you be encouraged by the transformative and redeeming power of his love. May you be met with the indescribable kindness of his heart as you look to him.

Savior, nothing compares to knowing you. Your leadership is loving and faithful. You are loyal and you are powerful. You are reliable in mercy, and the freedom I have found in you is unmatched. Thank you.

Wonderful Christ

I continually long to know the wonders of Jesus and to experience the overflowing power of his resurrection working in me. I will be one with him in his sufferings and become like him in his death.

Knowing Christ is a lifelong pursuit. We don't arrive at fullness of understanding this side of heaven. No mind can comprehend the magnitude of God's power or the richness of his love. As Paul says in 1 Corinthians 2:9, "This is why the Scriptures say: Things never discovered or heard of before, things beyond our ability to imagine—these are the many things God has in store for all his lovers."

What a beautiful journey we have ahead of us. What an amazing opportunity we have, even now, to know God more and more. Our hearts and minds expand in his limitless love. Every revelation is an awakening to his greatness. Whether we are in the deepest valley or standing on the tallest mountain, we are propelled by the longing to know the wonders of Christ's resurrection power in our lives. He is with us continually, and he is working in us to reveal himself.

Glorious Lord, I long to know you more than I can express. Bring revelation to my heart and expand my understanding in the glory of your love. You are wonderful.

Through Every Season

Be cheerful with joyous celebration in every season of life.
Let your joy overflow!

PHILIPPIANS 4:4

Remember that when Paul wrote these words of exhortation and encouragement to his friends, he was sitting in a prison cell. He would not instruct them to do what he was not already practicing in his own life. If Paul could find reason to joyously celebrate Christ in the confines of his imprisonment, then we can also experience joy, even in seasons of suffering.

How could we shift our mindsets by rejoicing in the Lord with us in our suffering? Paul and Silas sang songs of joy within their prison cell even after being beaten for preaching the gospel. What happened in their joy? The prison doors opened. Sometimes joy is the gateway to our deliverance. Let's not give up celebrating the power of Christ available to us every moment, in every circumstance. He is always worthy of our praise.

Worthy One, I choose to rejoice in you today. I celebrate your goodness present with me. Thank you for the power of your Spirit that liberates the captive and heals the wounded.

Withholding Nothing

Don't be pulled in different directions or worried about a thing. Be saturated in prayer throughout each day, offering your faith-filled requests before God with overflowing gratitude. Tell him every detail of your life.

PHILIPPIANS 4:6

D o you find yourself being pulled in different directions? Do you struggle to know where to focus your attention? Has worry overtaken your thoughts, keeping you up at night? Paul gives a focused suggestion to put our energies: "Be saturated in prayer…" We can offer God every single detail of our lives, not withholding anything from him.

God is the one who sees it all clearly. He doesn't miss a nuance or a stray hair. He takes in every detail. He cannot be surprised or ambushed. He is not worried or dismayed. Let's offer our faith-filled requests to God with hearts overflowing with gratitude. He not only sees us, but he also knows us. He loves us. He is faithful. He is worthy of our trust. He is more than able to deliver us from our fears. He is our Redeemer, and he will not fail.

Jesus, I lay my heart open before you. I will share every detail of my life with you, for you are trustworthy, merciful, and understanding. I trust you with it all. I love you, Lord.

Focused in Faith

Keep your thoughts continually fixed on all that is authentic and real,
honorable and admirable, beautiful and respectful, pure and holy,
merciful and kind. And fasten your thoughts on every glorious work
of God, praising him always.

PHILIPPIANS 4:8

A myriad of distractions can lead us from focused faith
throughout our days. Outside of our responsibilities and
family life, there is oversaturation of information and opinions
through many different forms of media. Let's take this opportunity to build boundaries around our thought life and focus on the
glorious kingdom of Christ.

When we bring our thoughts back to what is "authentic and
real, honorable and admirable, beautiful and respectful, pure
and holy, merciful and kind," we fix our minds on the fruit of the
Spirit. The more we train our minds to look for these qualities, the
more readily we will spot them. Discernment grows in this envi-
ronment, being able to differentiate between the values of God's
kingdom and the values of this world.

Faithful One, help me as I work to look for your qualities in this
world. Give me wisdom and discernment to guide my decisions and
my downtime. I want to know you more, to reflect your mercy, and
to experience your power in my life.

Overcomers

I'm trained in the secret of overcoming all things, whether in fullness or in hunger. And I find that the strength of Christ's explosive power infuses me to conquer every difficulty.

PHILIPPIANS 4:12–13

When we learn to be satisfied in Christ in every circumstance, what happens in, around, or to us can no longer dictate our peace. When the overwhelming abundance of God's presence with us is our place of rest, we are never without it. His presence is our home, and we can know his peace that passes understanding in every trial and trouble.

Whether we find ourselves in seasons of lack or in seasons of plenty, we have the explosive power of Christ to infuse us at every turn. We are never without the mercy of Christ. We are never without his loyal love covering us completely. We have more than all we need in the sufficiency of Christ in us. In all things, in all circumstances, "God has made us to be more than conquerors, and his demonstrated love is our glorious victory over everything" (Romans 8:37).

Resurrected One, it is in your life that I find myself coming alive. Your power is purer than the strength of the earth's kingdoms. I am yours, Lord, and I will worship you and follow you all the days of my life. You are my victory.

Secret Treasures

Your faith and love rise within you as you access all the treasures of your inheritance stored up in the heavenly realm. For the revelation of the true gospel is as real today as the day you first heard of our glorious hope, now that you have believed in the truth of the gospel.

COLOSSIANS 1:5

There are treasures of hope at hand today. The riches of revelation of Christ's kingdom are within reach. The power of the gospel is as potent right now as it was when we first heard. It's as powerful as when the early church heard it. The Spirit of God, filled with the power of God, is the same yesterday, today, and forever.

The treasures of truth are found in fellowship with Christ through his Spirit. We find the richness of his kingdom is exemplified through his Word. Faith and love rise within us as we experience the clarity of God's grace poured into our lives. A never-ending exchange of mercy and gratitude exists between the heart of God and our hearts in response.

Spirit, thank you for the treasures of pure mercy that you reveal to my heart and mind through fellowship with you. My faith increases as I witness your faithfulness over and over again.

Reason for Existence

For in him was created the universe of things, both in the heavenly realm and on the earth, all that is seen and all that is unseen...it all exists through him and for his purpose!

COLOSSIANS 1:16

Paul calls Jesus Christ "the firstborn heir of all creation" (Colossians 1:15). Before anything was made, he already existed. Everything, both now and always, finds its total completion in him. It is almost too much to imagine—the fullness of Christ. He is the source of the universe, all that is seen and unseen. Everything that lives, breathes, and moves exists through Christ.

He is our reason for existence. We live for his purposes. In Christ, we come alive in new ways, being born again of his kingdom. As we go through our days, whatever season we may find ourselves in, let's look to Christ for understanding, for purpose, and for belonging. He calls us his own, and he welcomes us with open arms ready to receive our curiosity and our questions. The one who created us can handle anything we bring to him.

Lord Jesus, I won't hamper my questions with fear of being misunderstood by you. You know me better than anyone else, and I believe that I find my reason, my purpose, and my hope in you.

Original Intent

By the blood of his cross, everything in heaven and earth is brought back to himself—back to its original intent, restored to innocence again!

COLOSSIANS 1:20

We find our fullness, our completion, in fellowship with Christ. He is the richness of God, and we are whole in him. His redemptive work was not only for us but also for all creation. His sacrifice on the cross accomplished reclamation for our souls and for the natural world.

Romans 8:20–21 says, "With eager expectation, all creation longs for freedom from its slavery to decay and to experience with us the wonderful freedom coming to God's children." We still wait for the fullness of this freedom. When Christ returns, he will set everything right once and for all. Until that day, we make ourselves at home in him, living for his kingdom and reveling in the mercy that has declared us pure in the Father's sight.

Faithful Father, until we see the fullness of your kingdom come to earth, there is a tension in the waiting. In this place, may your Spirit encourage, strengthen, and transform me in your incredible mercy. You have restored my innocence and called me pure and acceptable in your eyes. Thank you.

Awakened to Understand

We preach to awaken hearts and bring every person into the full understanding of truth. It has become my inspiration and passion in ministry to labor with a tireless intensity, with his power flowing through me, to present to every believer the revelation of being his perfect one in Jesus Christ.

COLOSSIANS 1:28–29

There is no better news than the exceedingly good news of the gospel. Paul states in the previous verses that there is a divine mystery being unfolded and manifested for every believer to experience. "Living within you is the Christ who floods you with the expectation of glory!" (v. 27).

In this awakening happening within our hearts, we begin to understand how much hope there is in Christ and his kingdom. His love is limitless and pure. It is unbiased and overflowing. The glory of God is more impressive than we can imagine. Whenever we catch a glimpse of his unfettered glory, our hearts are flooded with awe and wonder. He is so much better than we can conceive, and he reveals himself when we look for him.

Glorious God, I want to know you more than I do, more than I have. Increase my understanding of your incomparable goodness as you reveal fresh revelation and mercy to my heart, mind, and understanding. I look to you.

Wrapped in Comfort

I am contending for you that your hearts will be wrapped in the comfort of heaven and woven together into love's fabric. This will give you access to all the riches of God as you experience the revelation of God's great mystery—Christ.

COLOSSIANS 2:2

We cannot escape pain in this life. We can't avoid loss either. Life is full of transitions, changes, and endings. It is also full of new beginnings. Are we fixating on escaping the discomfort we feel when we are disappointed or discouraged? Avoidance is a coping mechanism, but it does nothing to deal with the underlying pain.

Christ is our ever-close comfort. His promises are sure, and his faithfulness will never diminish. In our suffering, God promises to hold us close. His Spirit wraps around us and embraces us with the liquid love of his presence. Our hearts are woven into the very fabric of his mercy-kindness. May we find our relief in him. When we are filled with sorrow, the Spirit draws near to us with the respite of his pure kindness.

Lord, be my comfort when I am filled with grief. Be my solace when I am sad. Wrap around me with the tangible peace of your presence and relieve the weight of my pain.

Riches of Revelation

For our spiritual wealth is in him,
like hidden treasure waiting to be discovered—
heaven's wisdom and endless riches of revelation knowledge.

COLOSSIANS 2:3

Whatever financial state you are in today, know that you have the riches of spiritual wealth in Christ. There is costly wisdom, abundant revelation, priceless hope, and overwhelming joy in his presence. He has more in his storehouses than we could ever deplete.

Proverbs 8:11 says, "Wisdom is so priceless that it exceeds the value of any jewel. Nothing you could wish for can equal her." Nothing. No earthly wealth or privilege satisfies the way that pure wisdom does. Let's sow into the bounty of the kingdom of Christ, relying on his endless resources to replenish us. We give out of the overflow of his abundance, and he pours more into us. What a wonderfully generous God we have.

Gracious One, I want to know the surpassing goodness of your glory. I don't want to live for my comfort but for the increase of your love, doing good at every turn. Guide me in your priceless wisdom.

Overflowing Fullness

Our own completeness is now found in him. We are completely
filled with God as Christ's fullness overflows within us. He is the
Head of every kingdom and authority in the universe!

COLOSSIANS 2:10

The wisdom of Christ's kingdom is better than the humanistic
judgments and arguments of this world. His ways are purer
than the systems of this world and its governments. His power is
pure and untainted by greed. He is love incarnate, and his mercy
flows through everything he does.

Christ is the only one who can complete us. He fills us
with his love, making our understanding of ourselves clearer.
No person can meet the needs that they cannot see. Christ sees
every need and desire within us, and only he can exceed our
expectations at every single turn. He meets our needs with the
overflowing fullness of his kindness. Let's open up to him, and
let's lay down every expectation of perfection from anyone else—
including ourselves.

*Great God, thank you for filling me with yourself. I trust you to
perfectly meet the needs that other people have left unmet. You
know me best. Awaken my heart in your life-light and heal every
wound with your love.*

Cancelled Debt

> He canceled out every legal violation we had on our record and the old arrest warrant that stood to indict us. He erased it all—our sins, our stained soul—he deleted it all and they cannot be retrieved!
>
> COLOSSIANS 2:14

In Christ, we have been forgiven of every wrong that we committed. That does not remove the natural consequences we may still have to deal with in our lives, but there is grace for that. Psalm 103:12 says, "Farther than from a sunrise to a sunset—that's how far you've removed our guilt from us." In the eyes of the Father, we are completely new in Christ. He holds nothing against us.

We have been embedded with Christ's mercy through the cross and his resurrection life. What God does not hold against us, may we never hold against ourselves. We get to choose today, and every day from here on out, how we will live and whom we will serve. May we live in the freedom of being a new creation in Christ, and may we proclaim his restorative and redemptive power to all who will listen.

Savior, thank you for canceling my debt and for making me new in your resurrection power. Your Word has the final say over my life, and my identity is firmly planted in your view of me. I will stand tall in this liberty.

Symphony of Grace

We receive directly from him, and his life supplies vitality into every part of his body through the joining ligaments connecting us all as one. He is the divine Head who guides his body and causes it to grow by the supernatural power of God.

COLOSSIANS 2:19

Not only does Christ's life supply our strength, but it also draws out the beautiful melody of his divine symphony from our lives. We each are like an instrument in the orchestra of our God. Though our lives have unique expressions and sounds, we come together to produce a beautiful opus with the music of his kingdom.

The wisdom of God's kingdom provides the direction we need to play our part. Jesus is our orchestrator and our heavenly director. We look to him for the cues we need. Under his leadership, we look to him for when to wait and when to play. With every movement he makes, we know when to crescendo and when to quietly support others. What a beautiful picture this is of Jesus as our source and our leader.

Jesus, thank you for the part I play in your kingdom. You supply every signal to the nuances of life. I look to you through everything; teach me the excellent way of your kingdom.

Resurrection Power

Christ's resurrection is your resurrection too. This is why we are to yearn for all that is above, for that's where Christ sits enthroned at the place of all power, honor, and authority! Yes, feast on all the treasures of the heavenly realm and fill your thoughts with heavenly realities, and not with the distractions of the natural realm.

COLOSSIANS 3:1–2

Christ's resurrection is your resurrection too. What areas of your life are in need of the redemption power of God? Even what seems dead is not hopeless in God. Though we may grieve the loss of people, dreams, and hopes, the Lord is constantly working to restore what was lost. In the soil of our grief, he is sowing seeds of hope.

The resurrection power of Christ is the power that flows through his Spirit in the inner places of our hearts and lives. He is at work even when we cannot make sense of the dormancy of winter. He brings beautiful new life out of the ashes of our disappointment. May we find our hopes resurrected in his powerful love today.

Resurrected One, in your life, I come alive. In your power, I find that your love shines brightly. Your mercy restores to life what was dead, and you redeem what I thought was lost forever. Thank you.

Continually Renewed

> You have acquired new creation life which is continually
> being renewed into the likeness of the One who created you;
> giving you the full revelation of God.
>
> COLOSSIANS 3:10

We are made new in the image of Christ when we come to him at first. But that's not the end of the story. We are continually being renewed in him. His mercy meets us every moment. It will never run out. His grace empowers us each new day. Christ has not stopped his loyal love from working within us.

In the kingdom of God, our nationality, education, and economic status mean nothing. We cannot earn more of his favor or lose our identity in him. We are equals before him. As we are continually renewed into the living image of God, we become known by our kindness, compassion, and integrity. As we become more like him, we shed the old value systems of the world. Praise God for his mighty work of mercy in our lives.

Creator, thank you for continually renewing my heart in the waves of your mercy. Refresh my mind in your truth and rejuvenate my hope in your delighted joy.

Robed with Virtue

You are always and dearly loved by God! So robe yourself with virtues of God, since you have been divinely chosen to be holy. Be merciful as you endeavor to understand others, and be compassionate, showing kindness toward all. Be gentle and humble, unoffendable in your patience with others.

COLOSSIANS 3:12

The greatest call we have in the kingdom of God is to love one another well. When we purpose to understand others, letting compassion line our hearts, we open ourselves to a deeper experience of mercy. We should always show kindness to others no matter who they are or where they come from.

When we practice gentleness with others, being humble in our hearts, we lay down our need to be right and to lord it over another. Loving well is better than winning an argument. Practicing patience with others while keeping our hearts from offense is a practical way to keep us living in love. Virtue does not mean perfection, so even when we mess up, we have a fresh opportunity to seek restoration in love. There is so much grace.

Lord, your ways are so much better than ours. I want to be more like you in love, being humble, patient, and resolute in mercy-kindness. Thank you for your grace to do this.

Saturated with Beauty

Let every activity of your lives and every word that comes from your lips be drenched with the beauty of our Lord Jesus, the Anointed One. And bring your constant praise to God the Father because of what Christ has done for you!

COLOSSIANS 3:17

When we simplify our focus and resolutely live to reflect the beauty of Jesus in all we do and say, things become clearer. If we lead with the purity of Christ's love in mind, then we can more clearly decide if something we are about to do or say will either hinder or promote that. Jesus is full of grace and mercy for everyone.

What a beautiful Savior he is. He experienced suffering and pain, as well as joy and belonging. He lived the full human experience, and he relates to us in our struggles. Nothing escapes his understanding. He loves us well, setting us free from the chains of sin and death that hung over us, and he liberates us to follow his merciful lead. Let's walk in the beauty of his ways today.

Jesus, I love you more than I can say. You have been so good to me, and I honor your liberating love in my choices today. I choose to reflect your kindness, your truth, and your compassion.

Walk in Wisdom's Steps

Walk in the wisdom of God as you live before the unbelievers,
and make it your duty to make him known.

COLOSSIANS 4:5

To walk in the wisdom of God is to walk in the light of his kingdom's values. James 3:17 puts it this way, "the wisdom from above is always pure, filled with peace, considerate and teachable. It is filled with love and never displays prejudice or hypocrisy in any form." The wisdom of God reflects the character of God—always.

The wisdom of God is not defined by harsh stances or pride in our theology. It is humble, and the heart that yields to the wisdom of God is also willing to yield to others. Is the wisdom we follow filled with peace? Is it considerate and teachable? If not, then it may not be the wisdom of God but rather the wisdom of the world. Let's look at the fruit and see.

Wise God, no one sees, knows, and understands more than you do. You are the source of everything. I trust you, and I choose to follow your kingdom ways even though it is not the natural thing to do. You are better than any system in this world.

Gracious Clarity

Let every word you speak be drenched with grace and tempered with truth and clarity. For then you will be prepared to give a respectful answer to anyone who asks about your faith.

COLOSSIANS 4:6

When we speak with compassion, drenched with grace, our words disarm offense. This is how God speaks to us—with kindness, truth, and clarity. He does not pacify us in our wrong thinking, but he does reveal truth wrapped in love. It is not weak to be gracious. It is bold to choose to reflect God's likeness in our gentle approach.

If we are accustomed to being berated when we have messed up, then a gentle correction may startle us. God does not lie in wait to surprise us with his anger. He is patient and kind, merciful and true, just and strong. Even as his wisdom brings clarity to our understanding, we can choose to partner with him in speaking the truth. When we are clear in our communication, it is an act of kindness.

Generous Father, thank you for the kindness of your correction. When I have a hard truth to share, help me to remain compassionate and kind, while still speaking the truth clearly. Thank you.

Practical Faith

We remember before our God and Father how you put your faith into practice, how your love motivates you to serve others, and how unrelenting is your hope-filled patience in our Lord Jesus Christ.

1 THESSALONIANS 1:3

Our faith is expressed in the outworking of love and hope in our lives. Faith isn't just a belief system that informs our ideals. It is also a value system that motivates and informs our choices. If we truly believe that Christ is the Son of God, that his sacrifice is sufficient, and his resurrection power still moves today, then our lives will reflect it.

Are there any areas of your life where you can put your faith into practice? How willing are you to serve others in love? How unrelenting is your hope-filled patience? Lean into the presence of the Lord, asking him to shine the light of his revelation-truth in your heart and mind. His wisdom will guide you and show you specific areas where you can practice putting your faith into action.

Spirit of God, you are my gracious help at all times. I invite your presence to fill me once more with the lavish love of your heart. Show me where I can stretch my faith and put it into practical action. Thank you.

Power of the Gospel

Our gospel came to you not merely in the form of words but
in mighty power infused with the Holy Spirit and deep conviction.
Surely you remember how we lived our lives transparently
before you to encourage you.

1 THESSALONIANS 1:5

The gospel of Jesus Christ is not simply a treatise to win over
our minds. The truth of Christ's sacrifice and resurrection is
not an argument to be won. The power of the gospel is displayed
through the miraculous might of the Holy Spirit. An intellectual
understanding falls short of the deep conviction of our hearts,
moved by the Spirit of God within us.

God is a gracious Father. He welcomes us as we are. He welcomes our questions as well as our praises. He does not demand
a perfect faith. He plants the seeds of faith within our hearts, and
his Spirit waters them. We don't rely on our own understanding
but on the revelation-knowledge of God that brings conviction of
the truth of his kingdom. Where there is living faith, there is the
power of God at work.

*Father, thank you for the power of your Spirit at work in the world
and in my life. You implanted the seeds of faith at first, and I look to
you to grow them in your garden of glory.*

Our Deliverer

> Now you eagerly expect his Son from heaven—
> Jesus, the deliverer, whom he raised from the dead
> and who rescues us from the coming wrath.
>
> 1 THESSALONIANS 1:10

Jesus is our deliverer. He is the hope of every nation, every community, and every heart. He will not abandon us in our need. We look ahead to the hope of his return, for he has promised that he will come back. His resurrection power is the source of our transformation. We don't wait in vain, and his Spirit's presence to heal, restore, and transform is the seal of his promise to us.

Where there is repentance, lives are changed. We turn wholeheartedly to God, leaving behind the idols of our former lives. Anything that kept us in fear or shame, any sin cycle or path to self-destruction, we can leave behind in the mercy of Christ. Our deliverer sets us free to live with his kingdom's purposes in sight, leading with love and pursuing peace.

Liberator, I eagerly wait for the day when you will return and I see you face-to-face. Until then, continually transform me with the power of your Spirit's presence within me. I long to know you more and more until you are my highest vision.

October

Pure Motivation

We have been approved by God to be those who preach the gospel.
So our motivation to preach is not pleasing people but pleasing God,
who thoroughly examines our hearts.

1 THESSALONIANS 2:4

What does a pure motivation look like before God's eyes? Is it not out of love, out of gratitude to God, and from an understanding of abundant grace? Only God can read our hearts. Only he knows what moves us. He knows when we are motivated by the craving of approval from others and when we are striving for recognition.

God has no hidden intent in his heart, and he has no desire or need to manipulate or cajole us into doing his will. He gives us freedom to choose how we will live. When we submit to his heart, we yield our lives to his kingdom ways—not because we have to but because it is our joy to. His ways are better, purer, and more powerful than the ways of this world's systems. May our hearts be motivated to please God more than trying to please anyone else. Psalm 136:1 says, "He is good, and he is easy to please!"

Gracious One, purify my motives in your love. I want to live for your pleasure more than any other's. I love you.

Wholehearted Reception

This is why we continually thank God for your lives, because you received our message wholeheartedly. You embraced it not as the fabrication of men but as the word of God. And the word continues to be an energizing force in you who believe.

1 THESSALONIANS 2:13

When we receive the message of the gospel of Christ wholeheartedly, it is an energizing force that fuels our passion. The Spirit of God enters our hearts, making his home within us and empowering us to live with all the fruit of God's kingdom.

Can you make more space for God in your heart today? Is there anything that has held you back from receiving the full mercy that God offers you? There is always more to experience, more to understand, and more to receive from the life force of the Holy Spirit. The kingdom of God is abundant and ever-expanding. Love is not a limited resource. Open up to the Lord and welcome him in, and he will fill the cracks of your understanding. Turn your attention to him, and he will meet you with the power of his presence.

Jesus, above every other thing, I believe that you are God. I believe that you fill my life with miracles of your mercy. Weave your love through the frayed edges of my story and reveal the power of your presence to me again.

Encouraged

So, our dear brothers and sisters,
in the midst of all our distress and difficulties,
your steadfastness of faith
has greatly encouraged our hearts.

1 THESSALONIANS 3:7

We are made for relationship. In verse 6 of this chapter, Paul says that Timothy "informed us that you hold us dear in your hearts and that you long to see us as much as we long to see you." This was the statement that preceded the encouragement that Paul speaks of experiencing. We were made to be seen and known, to be remembered and to be engaged with in love.

Can you recall a time when you were discouraged and the faithfulness of a friend brought hope, relief, and encouragement to your heart? Sometimes we overlook the simple ways we can connect with one another that may bring comfort. Take some time to reach out to someone you love whom you haven't talked with in a while. It may be just the encouragement they need.

Faithful Father, you are more steadfast than anyone. You are loyal in love, and you never overlook a hurting heart. As I reach out to encourage others today, may I also be filled with the relief of your love.

So Much Joy

How could we ever thank God enough for all the wonderful joy
that we feel before our God because of you?

1 THESSALONIANS 3:9

In the devoted company of faithful friends, we are encouraged. What joy is ours when those we love succeed! How much delight we experience when our friends and family faithfully follow the path of God's love in their lives. We have no need to manage or control the choices that others make, but we can certainly encourage and celebrate with those who are persevering in faith.

Who brings you joy when you think of them? Reach out and let them know today. Whose faith encourages your own? Write a note or make a call to them; perhaps it will uplift them the way that they have uplifted you. Whatever brings deep joy, tune into today and look for ways to spread it to others.

Jesus, thank you for the never-ending well of your joy. I'm so grateful for the abundance of delight I experience in relationship with others. May it bubble up even more today and spill over into the lives of those around me.

Continual Increase

May the Lord increase your love until it overflows toward one another and for all people, just as our love overflows toward you.

1 THESSALONIANS 3:12

Love is not a limited resource. It is ever expanding and ever flowing. This means that in every moment, we have access to more of it. Paul's prayer that the readers would experience the increase of the Lord's love in their lives had a direct focus—that it would overflow toward other people. God's mercy moves us toward one another. His compassion melts our defenses and compels us to connect to others.

Where we have experienced a lack of kindness, there is more love to draw from in Christ. An ever-increasing flow of mercy to drink from. When our own inner wells are filled with God's compassionate love, we give from his own overflow in our hearts to one another. However empty we may feel, the Lord offers us the abundance of his love to fuel us in acts of mercy.

Merciful Father, thank you for your limitless love that is continually poured over my life. Fill me with more today so that I may give from a place of overflow.

Dig In

Now, beloved brothers and sisters, since you have been mentored by us with respect to living for God and pleasing him, I appeal to you in the name of the Lord Jesus with this request: keep faithfully growing through our teachings even more and more.

1 THESSALONIANS 4:1

Faith in God and in his kingdom is not stagnant. May we remember that learning is a lifelong endeavor. This is true in every area of our lives—how much more in our journeys of faith? There is always more to learn, so let's not grow complacent.

What a wonderful opportunity we have to dig into the Word of God and to drink deep from the fellowship of the Holy Spirit. May we embrace this moment and turn our hearts and attention to the one who sticks closer than a brother. He is our faithful friend, our compassionate comforter, our wise teacher, and our ever-gracious guide through the terrain of this life. May we find his mercy sewn into the fabric of our lives as we meditate on the teachings of Christ through his Word.

Righteous One, awaken my heart to the truth of your kingdom and to the deep wisdom of your words. Continue to teach me what you are like and how to live in your likeness. Thank you.

Call to Holiness

God's call on our lives is not to a life of compromise and perversion but to a life surrounded in holiness.

1 THESSALONIANS 4:7

God has called us to live holy lives, reflecting the values of his kingdom. Living with integrity benefits us. When we live with kindness, honor, humility, and mercy in our interactions with others, we don't leave much room to compromise.

Let's remember that God sees our hearts and thoughts. He is not scandalized by them, nor is he impressed by them. In every moment, we can invite the gracious light of his Spirit to shine on our thought life and reveal areas that need his liberating love to overcome our conditioned responses. He is full of mercy, and his passion will purify our hearts as we yield to him.

Holy God, thank you for the help of your Spirit that transforms my heart and mind in the purity of your love. I yield my heart, mind, body, and very life to you. I am holy because you have made me holy. I will walk in your virtuous ways.

Conduits of Kindness

Indeed, your love is what you're known for throughout Macedonia. We
urge you, beloved ones, to let this unselfish love increase
and flow through you more and more.

1 THESSALONIANS 4:10

We present divine love through unselfishly choosing to
love one another just like Christ loves us. Jesus is our
ultimate example of what it means to choose a life of lived-out
mercy. His Spirit-life within us empowers us to choose his ways,
to follow in his footsteps.

How does kindness flow through your life? Christ is endlessly
kind to us. He is more gracious than we sometimes allow for,
especially when we want to put limits on how far his love will go.
The truth is that his love never recedes; it is never interrupted. It
increases, flowing unceasingly from his very being. Let's feast on
his love, filling up on the kindness of his heart toward all, and let's
become conduits of his kindness, releasing it in our own lives.

*Jesus, thank you for the limitless love that you shower over us. It is
more powerful than shame, fear, or even death. I choose to move in
compassion and kindness, reflecting your mercy in my relationships.*

Driving Ambition

Aspire to lead a calm and peaceful life as you mind your own business and earn your living, just as we've taught you.

1 THESSALONIANS 4:11

When we make living with integrity our goal, keeping our promises and following through on our word, we reflect the values of God's kingdom. Faithfulness and perseverance go hand in hand. Promoting peace and focusing on what is ours to do without meddling or micro-managing is honorable. Life can be much simpler when we center our lives around the important elements of the kingdom of Christ.

What is the driving ambition of your present season? How does that play out in your day-to-day life? Do your aspirations reflect the teachings of Christ? Do they cultivate the fruit of the Spirit in your relationships? It's okay to have simple aspirations, and it's okay for them to shift with the seasons. No matter what, if you are seeking peace, moving in love, and living to know Christ more, then you will find these fruits in your life.

Great God, you are the keeper of my days, and I trust you to help me walk through this life with grace and grit. As I build my life around the simplicity of your gospel, I rely on your strength to empower me when life is not easy. I trust you.

Children of the Light

You, beloved brothers and sisters, are not living in the dark,
allowing that day to creep up on you like a thief coming to steal.

1 THESSALONIANS 5:4

Though troubles come like storms sweeping through our lives, when we remain firmly rooted in Christ, we will not be shaken. We don't know when the tide of the world's favor will shift, and we can't predict when all that we have gained may be lost. Disaster strikes without warning, but those who are planted in the kingdom of Christ know that God is faithful, regardless of our present circumstances.

When we fix our eyes on Jesus, the one who called us and who continues to lead us through the twists and turns of this life, we turn ourselves to the source of light and understanding. Let's remain alert and clearheaded, knowing that no matter our situations, there is hope in the Lord. He is our firm help. Let's encourage each other to be courageous as long as it is called today, and let's continue to look to Jesus for all that we need.

Christ Jesus, thank you for your living light that shines through your presence. Thank you for the Scriptures that illuminate who you are. May I live as awake and aware to what you are doing. I rely on you.

Alert with Clarity

Since we belong to the day, we must stay alert and clearheaded
by placing the breastplate of faith and love over our hearts,
and a helmet of the hope of salvation over our thoughts.

1 THESSALONIANS 5:8

With clear vision of our mission in this life, and with faithfulness and love protecting our hearts, we are set apart with the shield of the hope of everlasting life in Christ's kingdom. Has our vision become fuzzy or muddled? Have we forgotten the purpose of this life? May we recalibrate in the presence of God's Spirit today, remembering who we are, what we have been called to, and how we can faithfully follow the steps of the Lord.

The Holy Spirit is our close confidant. The Spirit is the one who reveals the thoughts and purposes of Christ to us. Revelation runs deeper than knowledge. More than an acknowledgement of the truth, it is a conviction, a deeper understanding. Through Christ, we have the Spirit who reveals the perceptions of God. Let's give ourselves to deeper fellowship today. In this place, we can learn, grow, and develop in his wisdom.

Holy Spirit, may my mind be clear and focused on your clarifying truth. Reveal the perspective of Christ and direct me in how to live out his purposes in my life. You are my great teacher.

Wise Leadership

We appeal to you, dear brothers and sisters, to instruct those who are not in their place of battle. Be skilled at gently encouraging those who feel themselves inadequate. Be faithful to stand your ground. Help the weak to stand again. Be quick to demonstrate patience with everyone.

1 THESSALONIANS 5:14

Discernment helps us to recognize where people are out of place, either in their thinking or in their role. Perhaps they don't know where they belong, or they have simply lost focus of their place. When we recognize this, great humility is needed in our own hearts. Paul says to "be skilled at gently encouraging those who feel themselves inadequate" and to be quick to demonstrate patience with others.

Jesus was the ultimate servant leader. Paul, too, demonstrated the value of humbly presenting himself before others. Everyone is called to lead with love, whether it is one person or hundreds who look to us. With gentle encouragement, faithfulness to stand our ground, boldness to help the weak stand, and willingness to be patient, we reflect the wisdom of Christ's leadership in our own.

Great God, you are wiser than the most intelligent people of this earth. Your ways are true, and they do not lead us astray. I will stand on your mercy, and I will build my life on your kindness. May I reflect you in the way I relate to everyone.

Life of Gratitude

> Let joy be your continual feast. Make your life a prayer.
> And in the midst of everything be always giving thanks,
> for this is God's perfect plan for you in Christ Jesus.
>
> 1 THESSALONIANS 5:16–18

In every season of the soul, in every moment, we can feast on the unrelenting joy of the Lord. The Scriptures speak of the joy of the Lord being our very strength. When we are weak, the gracious delight of God is strong in us.

No matter what today holds, we can partake in the very present joy of the Lord. We can posture our hearts in prayer, no matter what we are doing. May our very lives become an unceasing prayer poured out to the one who breathed life into us in the first place. Let's practice gratitude in the rhythms of our day. Every turn of our attention is an opportunity to connect with the source of our joy, help, hope, and strength.

Jehovah, I taste your joy today as I turn my attention to your presence with me. I take this time not only to pray, but I also open my heart to you with the invitation of a never-ending conversation. Thank you for this day and thank you for being with me in it.

Unwavering Faith

We point to you as an example of unwavering faith for all the churches of God. We boast about how you continue to demonstrate unflinching endurance through all the persecutions and painful trials you are experiencing.

2 THESSALONIANS 1:4

What does unwavering faith look like? It is marked by perseverance. Unwavering faith does not give up in the face of hard times. It does not give in when our questions are more plentiful than our answers. Our faith is rooted in the character of God, and he is unchanging. It is not based on our experiences or on our own faithfulness. It is based upon the loyal love of God himself.

With unflinching hope in the nature of God, we can stand the trials and the pain that we experience in life. There *will* be hard times. This is not a reflection of God or his favor but rather of the world that we live in. How we go through the hard times shows where our faith, hope, and love ultimately lie. May we be those who persevere in kindness, integrity, and peace.

Unchanging One, I have built my faith upon your faithfulness. Your grace is my strength in the face of incredibly hard times. I know that you don't ignore my pain—you are with me in it. Thank you for your presence that helps me to endure whatever comes. You are good.

By His Power

With this in mind, we constantly pray that our God will empower you to live worthy of all that he has invited you to experience. And we pray that by his power all the pleasures of goodness and all works inspired by faith would fill you completely.

2 THESSALONIANS 1:11

Paul consistently offered prayers in his letters in order to encourage the readers. He did not simply say what he hoped for them; he partnered with God's heart over them and prayed that they would experience the fullness of Christ. Are we praying for those around us to experience the grace-strength of God to lead them into the fullness of their calling?

May we progress from being people who simply speak tropes over one another to people of intentional prayer and blessing. Let's sincerely encourage one another in our faith, doing whatever we can to help build each other up. Let's share in each other's sufferings and in our joys. Let's press on, in loving community, to take hold of the fullness of Christ.

Savior, you are the fullness that we are all looking for. You are the hope, the fulfillment, and the prize. I want to experience you more in my relationships. As I encourage others in sincerity and I receive encouragement from them, may our faith grow.

Beloved One

We always have to thank God for you, brothers and sisters, for you are dearly loved by the Lord. He proved it by choosing you from the beginning for salvation through the Spirit, who set you apart for holiness, and through your belief in the truth.

2 THESSALONIANS 2:13

Whatever this day has brought you so far, know this: you are dearly loved by the Lord. You have not disappointed him, and you have not disqualified yourself from receiving the riches of his mercy. Whether you awoke with joy in your heart or dread to face the day, you are fully and completely embraced by the love of God.

Dive into the riches of his presence, feasting on the fellowship of the Spirit who is with you. Ask for a fresh revelation of his kindness. Invite the wisdom of God to instruct you in the liberating ways of his kingdom. You have been set apart, hidden in Christ, and there is nothing more you need to do in this moment to receive the abundance of his compassion. Turn to him, for he is so very near.

Father, thank you for loving me so completely. In your mercy, I come alive. In your kindness, I find hope. Reveal your unceasing grace in new ways to me as I look to you today. Thank you.

Stand Firm

> So then, dear family, stand firm with a masterful grip of the teachings we gave you, either by word of mouth or by our letter.
>
> 2 THESSALONIANS 2:15

I t is important to remember the lessons we have learned throughout our journey of following the Lord. Wisdom does not have an expiration date, and the values of Christ's kingdom never grow stale. They are life-giving and true in every age and in every season.

The truth of Christ's living Word is the foundation of our very lives. When we align our lifestyles with the incomparable joy of following Christ, we will reap a harvest of his Spirit-fruit in our lives. There is more than enough peace, joy, patience, and kindness in the presence of God to produce lasting fruit. There is mercy that sustains us through the fiercest storms and unwavering peace that fills us with courage to face the battles that come our way. Christ is our firm foundation, and he will not be moved.

Lord Jesus, thank you for the wisdom of your Word that feeds my soul and teaches my heart to trust you. I build my life upon the foundation of your teaching, and I won't be moved from your merciful love that sustains me.

Inspired with Strength

Now may the Lord Jesus Christ and our Father God, who loved us and in his wonderful grace gave us eternal comfort and a beautiful hope that cannot fail, encourage your hearts and inspire you with strength to always do and speak what is good and beautiful in his eyes.

2 THESSALONIANS 2:16–17

There is a wellspring of life in the presence of our resurrected Savior and the Father of all. The Holy Spirit imparts the generous grace of God to our hearts, offering us comfort in our time of grief, hope in our despair, and strength in our weakness. We can find encouragement today in the embrace of his living love. There is more than enough for all that we need.

When we lean on the strength of God to fill us, it is his grace and mercy that inspire our hearts to follow in his ways. When we do what is good, speaking words of life, encouragement, and hope, partnering with his purposes, we produce beautiful fruit from lives that lead with love in all things. Integrity keeps us living in the light of Christ's kingdom. May we walk on the well-lit path of his love today, for he will never fail.

Living God, you are my beautiful hope and my eternal comfort. I depend on your presence to strengthen me in your love and to inspire me in strength. Thank you.

Appeal to Pray

Finally, dear brothers and sisters, pray for us that the Lord's message will continue to spread rapidly and its glory be recognized everywhere, just as it was with you.

2 THESSALONIANS 3:1

Paul did not hesitate to ask people to pray for him. Even more, his appeal for prayer was about more than just his well-being and those of his companions but for the spread of the gospel to go forth. In our prayer lives, how much time do we spend on our personal requests versus the spreading of the kingdom of God through the gospel message?

There is room for all sorts of requests in our prayer lives. God is not limited in his listening, and he hears every prayer we offer. In fact, it is important to have an open line of communication with him in order to deepen our intimacy with him. Even so, we cannot forget the priority of praying for his kingdom to come and his will to be done in the earth, even as it is in heaven. May we not neglect this part of the Lord's prayer.

Merciful One, forgive me for where I have been short-sighted in my prayer life. I want to partner with your kingdom. May your gospel spread rapidly and hearts embrace your truth.

Faithful Lord

The Lord Yahweh is always faithful to place you on a firm foundation
and guard you from the Evil One.

2 THESSALONIANS 3:3

What a beautiful God is the Lord Yahweh. We do not depend on our own strength, acumen, or ability to stand firm. God himself is the one who faithfully places us on the firm foundation of his love. He is the one who guards us from evil. When we turn to hide our lives in him, his mercy covers the unproductive and sinful ways of our past. He is our Redeemer, and he breathes new life into us.

Whatever we face, the Lord is faithful to set our feet on solid ground. Psalm 18:2 says, "Yahweh, you're the bedrock beneath my feet, my faith-fortress…my rock of rescue where none can reach me. You're the shield around me, the mighty power that saves me, and my high place." God himself is our foundation. He is our wrap-around shield. He is faithful to guard us, settle us, and keep us in himself.

Faithful Father, you are the hope of my heart. You are the one I depend on. You are my firm foundation, and I am found in you.

The Hope of the Messiah

Now may the Lord move your hearts into a greater understanding of God's pure love for you and into Christ's steadfast endurance.

2 THESSALONIANS 3:5

God's pure love is the place from which we grow into understanding of who he is, who we are, and what we're called to. We will never have a true understanding of the gospel without the pure love of God instructing our hearts, minds, and lives. It is not wasted energy to engage with the vast mercy of God, seeking to understand how truly great it is.

Love was what propelled Jesus to lay down his crown in order to take on flesh and bones, to be born a baby and to live out the human experience. Love led him to minister to the outcast as freely as to the people who followed Jewish custom. Love led him to the cross, where he surrendered to death on our behalf, and the power of his love is what resurrected him from the grave three days later. Whatever we do, may love lead us, teach us, and cover us. It is ever expansive and flowing from God's throne.

Savior, thank you for your love that flows from everything you do. You will not relent in mercy, and for that, I'm so grateful. Give me deeper understanding of your pure love as I look to you today.

Life of Worship

Brothers and sisters,
don't ever grow weary in doing what is right.

2 THESSALONIANS 3:13

When we offer ourselves as living sacrifices to the Lord, everything we do can be an expression of worship. As we give God glory through our activities, relationships, and conversations, our lives become seamless expressions of offering. With yielded hearts, we turn even ordinary activities into symphonies of praise to our wonderful Savior.

No humble act of love is insignificant. No choice to present honest truth, shrouded in kindness, is overlooked by God. He will honor every movement made in mercy. Let's not live to impress others, but let's live from deeply rooted hearts that are surrendered to Christ. He is worth every submission and sacrifice. He is worth every turn of our attention. He is worth it all.

Glorious Lord, there is nothing I could offer you that would impress you, and yet you delight in my sacrifice of praise. I choose to serve you through the mundane aspects of my day as much as through the interactions with those I admire. I want to please you more than I want to impress anyone else.

Lord of Peace

Now, may the Lord himself, the Lord of peace, pour into you
his peace in every circumstance and in every possible way.
The Lord's tangible presence be with you all.

2 THESSALONIANS 3:16

In God's presence, there is guidance, influence, and power to
transform our very lives. The peace of God is found in the presence of his Spirit with us, and it is tangible. It is not just an idea
to attain to. It is not a philosophy to embed in our minds. It is the
breath of God—the power of God.

Paul says in Philippians 4:6–7, "Tell him every detail of your
life, then God's wonderful peace that transcends human understanding, will guard your heart and mind through Jesus Christ."
The peace of God is found in fellowship with him. If you are
struggling to know peace today, turn to the Lord Jesus Christ who
is with you through his Spirit. Pour out your heart to him and
turn your attention to the goodness of his nature. The peace of his
presence is so very near.

*Prince of Peace, wrap around me with the tangible peace of your
presence even now. I rely on you more than anyone else. Do what
only you can do and bring relief, clarity, and confidence in your
faithful love.*

Sincere Faith

We reach the goal of fulfilling all the commandments when we love others deeply with a pure heart, a clean conscience, and sincere faith.

1 TIMOTHY 1:5

Faith is defined in Hebrews 11:1, as what "brings our hopes into reality and becomes the foundation needed to acquire the things we long for. It is the evidence required to prove what is still unseen." Faith is confidence of things hoped for and the conviction of things unseen. Our faith rests in confident trust of the faithfulness of God and in his unchanging nature.

We don't love others simply because it is the right thing to do. First John 4:19 says it this way: "Our love for others is our grateful response to the love God first demonstrated to us." We continue to choose to let love lead us because God first loved us. We give out of the overflow of his mercy in our lives. We choose to reflect his image in how we live. With a pure heart, clean conscience, and sincere faith, we reach the goal of fulfilling Christ's commandments.

Faithful One, I know that the choices I make will reflect my belief system. I want to reflect your loyal love. Fill me with your grace and revelation-knowledge that I may have more to offer.

Overflowing with Gratitude

My heart spills over with thanks to God for the way he continually empowers me, and to our Lord Jesus, the Anointed One, who found me trustworthy and who authorized me to be his partner in this ministry.

1 TIMOTHY 1:12

God is at work in our lives even if we have to dig a little to see it at the moment. How does his peace show up? Where does love meet us? Where have we experienced his kindness? His grace is available today to empower us in his strength. May we have eyes to see where his mercy weaves its thread through our lives.

Take a moment to look over your life. Invite the Spirit of God to show you where he has been at work in the details of your story. Where is his peace pouring out over you? As he reveals the fruit of his movement in your life, offer him gratitude from the overflow of your heart. Take some time to give thanks in a specific and authentic way.

Loving Lord, thank you for showing me where you are moving in my life in powerful ways. I'm so grateful that you never give up even when I don't recognize the work that you're doing. You're so wonderful.

Kissed by Mercy

Mercy kissed me, even though I used to be a blasphemer,
a persecutor of believers, and a scorner of what turned out to be true.
I was ignorant and didn't know what I was doing.

1 TIMOTHY 1:13

Mercy kisses the shame of our past, and it makes us new. Mercy's covering is the same for us all. It does not improve some and leave others wanting. We are completely new creations in Christ. Paul says this in 2 Corinthians 5:17: "If anyone is enfolded into Christ, he has become an entirely new person. All that is related to the old order has vanished…everything is fresh and new."

Paul was radically changed by the mercy of God and how it met him on the road to Damascus. He was never the same after his profound encounter with the Lord. Though how we come to the Lord is different for each of us, the effects of his mercy are the same. He loves us to life, making us new in him, cleaning our slates, and offering us the grace, peace, and pure pleasure of his presence. Hallelujah!

Merciful God, thank you for the power of your mercy that covers my shame and makes me pure and new in your sight. Your mercy brings me to life.

Flooded with Grace

I was flooded with such incredible grace, like a river overflowing its banks, until I was full of faith and love for Jesus, the Anointed One!

1 TIMOTHY 1:14

Just as Christ's mercy meets us all in the same abundant measure, so does his incredible grace. Overflowing grace floods us with faith and love for Jesus, our Savior. When we're running dry, he is the love that rains down on us and fills us up. There is an abundance of grace today for whatever we need.

Let's press into the presence of God and ask him for the strength we are lacking. He is not lacking, and he does not withhold good gifts from his children. The best gift he gives us is the gift of himself. He is our loving leader, our wise counselor, our close comfort, and our faithful friend. He is our powerful Savior, our ever-present help, and our perfect peace. He is all these things and more. What grace is ours in him!

Gracious God, thank you for the abundance of your presence in my life. I look to you when I am weak, and I look to you when I am strong. I always need you, Lord. Thank you for never turning me away.

Gripped by God

I was captured by grace, so that Jesus Christ could display through me the outpouring of his Spirit as a pattern to be seen for all those who would believe in him for eternal life.

1 TIMOTHY 1:16

Jesus came to bring sinners back to life. That is what Paul says in the preceding verse. He declares that he was the worst sinner of all, yet the glorious grace of God saved him. Our lives are testimonies of God's goodness. Christ's love led him to lay down his life to set the captives free. In him, we are free from the sin that once entangled us, and we are liberated from the curse of death.

Have you been captured by grace? Has his merciful grasp taken hold of your life and raised you from the ashes? Love kneels down and mercy gets in the dirt where we are. It cleans us off, picks us up, and makes us new. May you know the all-surpassing goodness of his mercy-kindness and be filled with the grace of his presence. It is better than you can imagine.

Wonderful Jesus, my life is yours. Pour your Spirit in, over, and through me. May I be a pure reflection of your living love and transformative mercy. Thank you for your wonderful grace.

King of Glory

Because of this my praises rise to the King of all the universe who is indestructible, invisible, and full of glory, the only God who is worthy of the highest honors throughout all of time and throughout the eternity of eternities! Amen!

1 TIMOTHY 1:17

Why do Paul's praises rise to the King of all the universe? Because he had been captured by the love of God, brought to life in his mercy, and flooded with super-abounding grace. For all these reasons, for the transformative power that God had worked in his life, Paul could not stop giving praise to God.

What is your testimony of God's work in your life? What has he done for you? May you find the floods of his mercy waters are great as you look for his fingerprints of love upon your life. God pursues you with an unrelenting passion. The King of glory is not finished working out his miracles of mercy in your life. Let your praises rise as you discover and uncover where he has been working all along.

Lord of lords, you are worthy of all the praise I could ever give you. I won't hold back my gratitude from you today. I won't be silent about how you have transformed my life in your living love. Keep doing what you do. I will keep praising you.

Keep Interceding

Most of all, I'm writing to encourage you to pray with gratitude to God. Pray for all men with all forms of prayers and requests as you intercede with intense passion.

1 TIMOTHY 2:1

I t is good practice to begin our prayers with gratitude. Psalm 100:2 says to "sing your way into his presence with joy!" Every time we pray, we connect to God the Father through Jesus. We enter into the presence of God through the Spirit. When we come with thanksgiving, we prime our hearts to see God as he is— larger than life.

Let's "come right into his presence with thanksgiving…for Yahweh is always good and ready to receive" us (Psalm 100:4, 5). No matter how today started, we can choose to approach him with gratitude now. In this place of fellowship, we see that God is "so loving that it will amaze" us and "so kind that it will astound" us (Psalm 100:5). What a wonderful encounter awaits us in the fellowship of his presence. As we continue to intercede, we touch his heart and partner with his purposes.

Gracious God, I come to you with joy, gratitude, and awe. Thank you for the love that you pour over your people. Thank you for hearing us, for caring for us, and for tending to our needs. Draw me closer to your heart in your presence.

Prayers for Peace

Pray for every political leader and representative, so that we would be able to live tranquil, undisturbed lives, as we worship the awe-inspiring God with pure hearts. It is pleasing to our Savior-God to pray for them.

1 TIMOTHY 2:2–3

Are our prayers for the leaders of our nations wasted? Paul says that "it is pleasing to our Savior-God to pray for them." If that is true, then we should not give up praying for them. We pray for their hearts to embrace his life and turn to the full knowledge of truth (v. 4). We also pray for wisdom over their decisions so that we may be able to live in peace.

Prayers for peace are never wasted. The peace of God is an important principle of his kingdom. And it is our promised companion through the ups and downs of this life. Tranquility in our communities and countries allows us to worship God freely, without fear. May we be people who pursue peace in our lives and with our prayers, not only for ourselves but for all people.

Beautiful Jesus, your peace is not easily upset, and you do not make a promise and then break it. You are better than politicians. Even so, I pray for the leaders of this nation, for my local government, and every level between. May there be peace in our homes, cities, and nations.

November

One True Leader

For God is one, and there is one Mediator between God
and the sons of men—the true man, Jesus, the Anointed One.

1 TIMOTHY 2:5

Though we pray for our worldly leaders, and we do this with hope and passion, as children of God, we know that our one true leader is Christ. He is the hope of the nations, as the prophet Isaiah spoke, the fulfillment of the law, as Jesus himself said in Matthew 5, and the joy of every heart.

Jesus does not deceive or manipulate us. He is the perfect representation of the Father. He is our "King-Priest...who rose into the heavenly realm for us, and now sympathizes with us in our frailty" (Hebrews 4:14). Let us look to him above every other, for he is our mediator. There is no one greater in the eyes of men or of God—we can trust him with everything.

King Jesus, my trust isn't in powerful people who can manipulate others with their prestige or money. My trust is in you. I will put my hope in you above every other, letting my faith be rooted in your faithfulness. Be glorified in my life and in the earth.

Frustration Free

I encourage the men to pray on every occasion with hands lifted to God in worship with clean hearts, free from frustration or strife.

1 TIMOTHY 2:8

Prayer is always a good idea. When we are frustrated, we can turn our energies and mindsets toward God, remembering how good he is, and partner with his truth. Worshiping God changes our outlook. We are transformed by God as we adore him, focusing our attention on his glorious nature.

Every occasion is an occasion for prayer. Paul says this numerous times. He tells the Ephesians to "constantly intercede with every form of prayer at all times" (6:18). He instructs others to "make your life a prayer" (1 Thessalonians 5:17). This message is repeated in so many different ways because it is our lifeline to the Lord. It is how we deepen our relationship with Jesus. May we take this encouragement to heart and pray at all times, in all ways, with our very lives.

Jesus, I will not let frustration drive me from prayer; rather, I will let it drive me to you. I give you my attention and my willingness to change. I worship you.

Spiritual Shepherds

An elder needs to be one who is without blame before others. He should be one whose heart is for his wife alone and not another woman. He should be recognized as one who is sensible, and well-behaved, and living a disciplined life.

1 TIMOTHY 3:2

Pastors and other leaders of the church should be well respected in their community. It is a noble ambition to aspire to be a pastor, and yet it is not for everyone. A pastor should be faithful to his or her spouse, level-headed and sensible, and in control of his or her life. Paul goes on to say that a pastor should also be able to teach, as well as be known for hospitality.

Pastors do not have an "in" with God more than any other. However, they are set apart to serve his church. This is not something to be taken lightly. Integrity and wisdom, faithfulness and devotion, are traits that serve a leader well. Gentleness and sobriety of mind are paramount to their leadership as shepherds of God's people. Whether or not we find ourselves drawn to this path, may we know the indicators of good leaders as characterized by God's Word.

Good Shepherd, thank you for being the perfect example of leadership. May my life be characterized by the traits of your kingdom as I mature in the soil of your mercy. Thank you.

Tested and Proven

He should be respected by those who are unbelievers, having a beautiful testimony among them so that he will not fall into the traps of Satan and be disgraced.

1 TIMOTHY 3:7

Continuing with the traits of a good church leader, Paul instructs that they should be respected not only within the body of believers but also by the larger community. Integrity is respected by people everywhere, whether they are believers or not. No one can argue with a person who does the right thing with humility, honesty, and care.

Have we passed through our wilderness journeys, being tested and proven? Though each of our lives winds through seasons of testing—even Jesus was tested in the desert—how we go through them determines our character. We are shaped and forged in the fires of our testing. May we lean on the grace of God, our ever-present help, to strengthen us, keep us, and transform us every step of the way.

Righteous One, may my character be refined in the heat of your fire, and may your close comfort and strength uphold me when I have nothing left to offer. I want to reflect your love more than anything else.

People of Our Word

> In the same way the deacons must be those who are pure
> and true to their word, not addicted to wine,
> or with greedy eyes on the contributions.
>
> 1 TIMOTHY 3:8

Jesus taught that we should be sober-minded, lovers of God and not of money. If we value wealth more than we value mercy, then we will be driven by and distracted by it. As believers we should be pure and true to our word, faithfully following through on what we said we would do. It is important to look for these traits especially in leaders, for they should be trustworthy.

In fact, Paul says that "each of them must be found trustworthy according to these standards before they are given the responsibility to minister" (v. 10). If we are looking to lead, we must first focus on building our character. No matter what roles we play in this life, the foundation of faithfulness and follow-through, honesty and humility, will be a steady place to build on.

Jesus, I don't want to be hasty in taking on leadership when you are still forging my character in the fires of your mercy. I trust you and your timing, and I know that being a person of integrity is more valuable than my job title.

Distinguished in Truth

The women also who serve the church should be dignified,
faithful in all things, having their thoughts set on truth,
and not known as those who gossip.

1 TIMOTHY 3:11

In the New Testament church, women served in ministry as well as men. Phoebe is an example of this. In Romans 16:1, she is mentioned as being "a shining minister of the church in Cenchrea." Certainly, we can find women serving the church in many different roles today, no matter the theology behind women in leadership. We find them teaching children, leading worship, speaking from the pulpit, and serving in various other capacities.

Regardless of the role, those who serve the church should be dignified, faithful to follow through, truth bearers, and truth tellers. In any other sphere, leaders reflect the values of the organization. In the church, this same principle applies. With hearts and lives devoted to the Lord, his law of love directs our steps and our growth. May we be living reflections of his heavenly kingdom on earth.

Lord, I'm so glad that in you there is no distinction between class, sex, or race. You see us all and welcome our participation. I want to reflect you in my life no matter what roles I fill. You are my great reward.

Mystery of Righteousness

For the mystery of righteousness is beyond all question! He was revealed as a human being, and as our great High Priest in the Spirit!

1 TIMOTHY 3:16

The great mystery of righteousness is ultimately the beautiful reality of Jesus Christ living within the believer. He is our great High Priest, our righteous King. There is no other God before him, and there is none greater.

Every knee will one day bow before the Son of Righteousness, and it is this same Messiah who makes his dwelling within us now through his Spirit. Ephesians 3:17 puts it eloquently: "By constantly using your faith, the life of Christ will be released deep inside you, and the resting place of his love will become the very source and root of your life." The love of Christ is our source, and it is so very near. We do not have to search far and wide, making pilgrimages to his presence. His presence is here, now, within us. What a glorious mystery.

King of kings, I can't rightly comprehend the wonders of your love, and yet you are constantly pouring over me with the rivers of your mercy. I turn my attention to you, Spirit, and am so grateful that you are near. Feed my soul with the nourishment of your truth.

Discernment Is Necessary

The Holy Spirit has explicitly revealed: At the end of this age,
many will depart from the true faith one after another,
devoting themselves to spirits of deception
and following demon-inspired revelations and theories.

1 TIMOTHY 4:1

When our roots grow deep into the soil of God's living Word, we are nourished by the waters of his wisdom. There is enough grace to cover our missteps, and his love will always bring us back to the reality of Christ's merciful nature.

In verse 3, Paul goes on to describe what some of this deception will look like: "They will require celibacy and dietary restrictions that God doesn't expect." In Christ, we are given true freedom to live in his love. This means we can eat without guilt, marry without shame, and live with compassion driving our service. God's love expands and liberates, while fear restricts. May our discernment be rooted in the peace and wisdom of God's merciful truth.

Redeemer, where fear seeks to keep me small, I choose to align with your love, where there is grace to move and even to make mistakes. I stand on the truth of your Word that says that I am free indeed, and there is no need to be restricted by man-made rules to please you. You are pleased with my yielded heart.

Celebration of Faith

We know that all creation is beautiful to God
and there is nothing to be refused if it is received with gratitude.

1 TIMOTHY 4:4

There is so much more liberty in God's grace than we could ever take advantage of. Grace does not overlook accountability, but it does break down needless walls that keep us distracted. We don't need to micromanage others' choices. When it comes to food, this means that if we are vegan, we don't have to convince others to become vegan. If we eat whole foods only, we are not better than others who choose differently.

Let us, with gratitude, gladly receive whatever it is that is before us without guilt. We don't all have to choose the same, and that's a gift. The celebration of faith is that we get to partake freely and not judge each other's choices in these matters. Whether it's food, media, clothing choices, or living styles, we can be ourselves and honor the Lord, for he knows our hearts.

Creator, I'm so glad that there is such diversity in your creation. I look at the flowers and the trees, the deserts and the mountains, and there is so much beauty and bounty. I freely live as you have created me, true to your purposes, my convictions, and your love.

Nurturing Grace

If you will teach the believers these things, you will be known as a faithful and good minister of Jesus, the Anointed One. Nurture others in the living words of faith and in the knowledge of grace which you were taught.

1 TIMOTHY 4:6

The principles of living by faith with the knowledge of God's generous grace applies to much more than what we eat. It advises every choice we make and how we move in the world. Paul says in verse 7 to "be quick to abstain from senseless traditions and legends" and to "instead be engaged in the training of truth that brings righteousness."

How does the focus of our faith line up with this? Are we distracted by traditions that we participate in just because it's what we've always done or because others we respect do it? Do we judge others based on their participation? The training of truth that brings righteousness is built upon the gospel of Christ. We live by faith, building our lives upon the mercy-kindness of God. We choose to extend compassion rather than judgment. We depend on the grace-strength of the Spirit to refine and fuel us. We live with surrendered hearts, and we believe that God is faithful and greater than our understanding.

Gracious God, where I have become distracted by things that take away from your liberating truth, show me. Shine the light of your love on the areas where I have gotten it all wrong. Thank you for grace.

Eternal Value

Athletic training only benefits you for a short season,
but righteousness brings lasting benefit in everything;
for righteousness contains the promise of life,
for time and eternity.

1 TIMOTHY 4:8

Training, whether we think of it in terms of pro-athletes or military boot camp, is an intense process. A tremendous amount of discipline goes into it. Athletes train their bodies to get in peak performance for their sport. Recruits go through rigorous training to get ready for the battlefield. They put a lot of effort in for a short season or deployment.

Training in righteousness also requires discipline and focus. It demands time and energy. But the benefits of righteousness extend to every area of life, even into the eternal promise of life in God's heavenly kingdom. We are saved by grace, and this will always be true. But the training of our souls in righteousness is for our benefit, both now and for his kingdom come.

Savior, I want my life to reflect your kingdom's values. I want righteousness to shine from every corner of my life. May I bring you glory, and may your grace satisfy every need I have.

Faithful and True

Don't be intimidated by those who are older than you; simply be the example they need to see by being faithful and true in all that you do. Speak the truth and live a life of purity and authentic love as you remain strong in your faith.

1 TIMOTHY 4:12

Age is neither a qualifier nor disqualifier of our faith. Whether young or old, we can either be faithful or unreliable. Paul's admonition to young Timothy was that he simply be an example by being faithful and true in all that he did. This is simple, but it is significant. When we speak the truth, live it with purity, and we demonstrate authentic love in all we do, we reflect the glory of God in our lives.

This is not to say that we can do this perfectly, but perfection is not the goal. Seeking restoration when we have wronged someone is a part of living a faithful and true life. Speaking the truth means humbling ourselves when we have erred. Living a life of purity means remaining free of shame and fear, living in the light of God's love before others. Let's keep it simple and leave intimidation behind.

Lord, I choose to live for you and your pleasure. Thank you for your grace that empowers me in faith. I love you.

Intention into Action

Make all of this your constant meditation and make it real with your life so everyone can see that you are moving forward.

1 TIMOTHY 4:15

When we recognize what God has already given us, the power of his love at work in our lives, there is no need to minimize his gracious mercy in order to appease others. May our testimonies and examples spur others on to take hold of God's mercy in their own lives.

As we go from knowledge of who God is into the practice of faith in action, we partner with his grace and live out his purposes. Paul goes on in verse 16 to say, "Give careful attention to your spiritual life and every cherished truth you teach, for living what you preach will release salvation inside you and to all those who listen." It is important to partner our beliefs with our lifestyles, living what we preach. If we claim to believe something and yet we don't live like it, we are pretenders. Let's be authentic and true, in our lifestyles as well as our speech.

Faithful One, may my life and words align. I know that integrity matters, and I want to be known as someone who lives what they believe. Thank you for your mercy that helps me.

Honorable Conduct

Don't be harsh or verbally abusive to an older man; it is better to appeal to him as a father. And as you minister to the younger men it is best to encourage them as your dear brothers.

1 TIMOTHY 5:1

A humble and gracious attitude goes a long way in our relationships. Even in correction, God is kind. Why should we be any different? It is honorable to make our appeals with encouragement and gentleness. Firm truth does not have to be communicated in a harsh way. The truth spoken in love reflects the heart of God.

Proverbs 15:1 warns against using sharp, cutting words, "Don't you know that being angry can ruin the testimony of even the wisest of men?" How we present the truth is as important as what we say. Let's take care how we speak to others, then, knowing that when we "speak healing words, [we] offer others fruit from the tree of life" (Proverbs 15:4). It is honorable when we treat others with love and respect even when we disagree with them.

Wise One, I know that your ways are better than the ways of this world. I choose to partner with your wisdom and your mercy. Help me to be kind even when it is a sacrifice to be so. Fill my heart with your compassion.

Like Family

Honor the older women as mothers, and the younger women,
treat as your dear sisters with utmost purity.

1 TIMOTHY 5:2

When we approach each other like family, as mothers and fathers, brothers and sisters, we reflect that we are a part of the family of God, the body of Christ. We are not strangers or acquaintances. We should honor each other in our humanity, looking through the lens of God's love.

Many cultures around the world treat their communities like extended family. Young people are to call the older women "aunties" or "big sister" out of respect. Unfortunately, we miss the communal care that often happens organically in these cultures because we are so individualized in the West. However, we can put this into practice in our faith community, honoring each other as family and not simply as familiar faces.

Father, thank you for setting us in the family of your kingdom. I want to know even deeper fellowship in the communal care of your church. I will not overlook the humanity of my brothers and sisters in Christ.

Pure Practice of Love

Timothy, in the presence of God and our Lord Jesus Christ, and before the chosen messengers, I solemnly charge you to put into practice all these matters without bias, prejudice, or favoritism.

1 TIMOTHY 5:21

All around us, people use a tremendous amount of bias to promote some over others. However, Paul charges Timothy to elect leaders of the church without using favoritism, prejudice, or bias. This is a tall order and one that goes against the world's ways.

When Samuel was going to anoint the son of Jesse, he automatically jumped to the conclusion that the strong warrior standing before him was to be the king of Israel. God, however, spoke to him and said, "The Lord does not look at the things people look at. People look at the outward appearance, but the Lord looks at the heart" (1 Samuel 16:7 NIV). Let's take the lead of the Lord, then, and look at the fruit of a person's character rather than the outer wrappings. May we honor others the same way that God honors them.

Yahweh, I want to look at others the way that you do, refusing to be impressed by power, prestige, or charm. You see through all of that to the motivations of a person's heart. May I value integrity and character more than charisma.

All Will Be Revealed

It is the same way with good works, even if they are not known at first,
they will eventually be recognized and acknowledged.

1 TIMOTHY 5:25

The fruit of our lives will become apparent not only to us but also to others. If we will keep planting seeds of righteousness, then we will harvest righteousness in our lives. If we sow seeds of bitterness, then bitterness is what we will reap. Paul says it this way in Galatians 6:7, "God will never be mocked! For what you plant will always be the very thing you harvest."

What we give our energy to, we will see in our lives. What we tend to will grow. Let's give our focus to fellowship with Christ, and let's give our attention to the values of his kingdom. Seeds of love, joy, peace, patience, kindness, and goodness are valuable crops in our lives. Faithfulness, gentleness, and self-control serve us well. Let us take our intentions and cultivate them with our actions in the soil of God's grace.

God, you are a skilled gardener, and I want my life to be full of your fruit. I yield to your leadership, and I submit to your pruning. Show me what needs to be removed and where I need to tend to my own garden, and I will do it.

Respecting Others

Instruct every employee to respect and honor their employers, for this attitude presents to them a clear testimony of God's truth and renown. Tell them to never provide them with a reason to discredit God's name because of their actions.

1 TIMOTHY 6:1

I t is important that we show respect to people no matter how we relate to one another. Employees should honor their employers. The golden rule goes in effect here as it does in all our interactions. We should treat each other the way we would like to be treated, out of kindness and consideration. When we show up to do a job, we should do it with all our attention, our skill, and to the best of our ability.

In the same way, employers should treat their employees with dignity. A kind and fair boss is a reflection of the Father. God's love is our barometer, not the standards of the world or even the industry that we find ourselves in. Let's not only do our work well but also may we treat those we work with respectfully.

Jesus, no one is worthy of more respect than you. Even though you were overlooked and mistreated, you still offered dignity and honor to others. I want to walk in your footsteps and see the deposits of your glory in every person I see.

Awe of God

If anyone spreads false teaching that does not agree with the healthy instruction of our Lord Jesus, teaching others that holy awe of God is not important, then they prove they know nothing at all!

1 TIMOTHY 6:3

Love and respect for God are important. There is more to the awe of God than these elements, though. When we live our lives in the awe of God, we take him at his Word, worshiping with the awareness of his holiness. Psalm 96:9 puts it this way, "Worship the Lord God wearing the splendor of holiness. Let everyone wait in wonder as they tremble before him."

When was the last time you waited in wonder before God? When was the last time you were overwhelmed by the holiness of his presence? Isaiah was overcome by the holy awe of God when he had an encounter with the cloud of glory in God's throne room, as described in Isaiah 6. When we encounter God's holiness, we cannot help but to recognize how great he is and how weak we are in comparison. He is majestic, powerful, and full of glorious light.

Jesus, you are the light of the world, and through you all the nations find their home. Reveal your glory to me so that I may be reminded of how great you are.

Heavenly Cravings

But those who crave the wealth of this world slip into spiritual snares. They become trapped by the troubles that come through their foolish and harmful desires, driven by greed and drowning in their own sinful pleasures. And they take others down with them into their corruption and eventual destruction.

1 TIMOTHY 6:9

Paul prefaces this statement by reminding us how our hands are empty when we come into the world, and when we leave this world, they will be empty again. That is to say, we brought nothing with us into this life, and we can't take any possessions when we leave it.

When we are driven by greed and lust for more, our appetites will never be satisfied. But we know that God is the source of every good thing. He is the only true and perfect fulfillment of our longings. All that we long for is what we ultimately find in him. Safety, security, belonging, connection—they are met in his glorious fellowship and in the abundance of his kingdom. May we turn toward heaven and feed the longings that push us in Christ's direction.

Lord, I redirect my focus to you again today. Meet me with your overwhelming mercy and reorient my mindsets in the truth of your kingdom. Thank you.

Clear Conscience

So now, I instruct you before the God of resurrection life and before Jesus, the Anointed One, who demonstrated a beautiful testimony even before Pontius Pilate, that you follow this commission faithfully with a clear conscience and without blemish until the appearing of our Lord Jesus Christ.

1 TIMOTHY 6:13–14

How do we keep our conscience clear? Is it by perfectly performing for others? Is it by being faultless in a world that is anything but? None of us is perfect, and we won't ever get it all right all the time. That's not the point of the gospel. We are to lean on the grace of God, the righteousness of Christ covering us, to be made new. The amazing part of this is that we are continually being made new in him. His mercies are new every moment. The power of his love is strong enough to cover every misstep we will ever make.

Christ is our freedom. He is our redemption. We come to the Father through what he has already accomplished—never on our own merit. Whenever we fall, we have an opportunity for restoration. Let's walk in the light of the Lord.

Lord Jesus, I follow your words, your will, and your ways. I'm so grateful for your faithful help every step of the way.

True Satisfaction

To all the rich of this world, I command you not to be wrapped in thoughts of pride over your prosperity, or rely on your wealth, for your riches are unreliable and nothing compared to the living God. Trust instead in the one who lavishes upon us all good things, fulfilling our every need.

1 TIMOTHY 6:17

Money can take you a lot of places in this world. It can garner favor from the powerful and open doors that otherwise would stay closed. However, prosperity in the world is not a reflection of favor with God. It is nothing compared to the riches we find in Christ.

Money can be gained, and wealth can be lost. It is unreliable. But the steadfast love of God is as reliable as the sunrise. It is larger than the breadth of the sky. It is deeper than the ocean. It is farther than the reaches of the farthest galaxy. If we are rich in anything, including wealth, may we be "rich in remarkable works of extravagant generosity, willing to share with others," as Paul says in verse 18. We reflect the generous kingdom of our good Father when we do.

Faithful One, you are the only one who truly satisfies my soul. I don't rely on the riches of this world to get me by. I choose to be generous as you are generous.

Even Greater

My beloved son, I pray for a greater release of God's grace, love, and total well-being to flow into your life from God our Father and from our Lord Jesus Christ!

2 TIMOTHY 1:2

J esus said in John 10:10, "I have come to give you everything in abundance, more than you expect—life in its fullness until you overflow!" What an amazing Redeemer he is, that he would offer us not only salvation for our souls but also the fullness of life through fellowship with him. He gives more than we expect. In that case, may we raise our expectations in him.

In the opening lines of this letter, Paul, in line with what Jesus proclaimed, prays for a greater release of all that God has to offer over Timothy. There is more available in Christ than we have yet experienced. There is more grace, more love, and an abundance of peace to fortify us. There is power to settle our fears and uplift our hopes in him. May we press in for the greater things of God's kingdom and pray for their release over others.

Jesus, you are greater than anyone can fathom. The riches of your mercy know no end. Flood my life with your goodness and fill my heart with your presence. I long to know you more.

Fan the Flame

I'm writing to encourage you to fan into a flame and rekindle the fire of the spiritual gift God imparted to you when I laid my hands upon you.

2 TIMOTHY 1:6

Do you have gifts that have lain dormant in your life? It is never too late to reawaken them. Remember the gifts that were ignited in your youth and fan them into flame. Spend some time thinking through the things in your life that you have poured your passion into and remember what has been imparted to you.

God is a generous giver. He is liberal with his love. If you struggle to know what your gifting is, look back at what brought you joy and what came easily in your youth. If you have had prophetic words, go over them and see what still resonates. Ask your friends and family what they know to be true of you. There are natural gifts and supernatural gifts, and both are important. Fan them into flame and rekindle the fire that God has put within you.

Generous Father, thank you for the gifts that you have given me. Remind me of the things that you have deposited in me that I may have forgotten about. Breathe your life-giving light, and I will fan the flame you ignited in me at first.

Know the Source

God will never give you the spirit of fear,
but the Holy Spirit who gives you mighty power, love, and self-control.

2 TIMOTHY 1:7

The fear of man is not from God. Intimidation tactics are not a tool of the kingdom. The Holy Spirit fills us with the gracious power of God, overflowing our tanks with his love, and he gives us the clarity of his wisdom that instructs us in self-control. Where fear tries to keep us small, God's Spirit moves us into the expanse of his grace.

Is there a move you've been hesitating to make? Is there a long-awaited dream that you have been second-guessing? Consider what doubts are holding you back. Are they driven by the fear of what others may think or by the Holy Spirit's wisdom to wait? Only you can know the difference, and you can trust your connection to the Spirit. His fruit is easy to spot, for where he moves, there is underlying peace. Lean into your source today and let love lead you.

Spirit, thank you that there is no fear of missing out in you. I trust your wisdom and your grace to guide me into your goodness. Breathe peace into my soul as I move ahead step by step. In you, I am never stuck.

Words of Healing

Allow the healing words you've heard from me to live in you
and make them a model for life as your faith
and love for the Anointed One grows even more.

2 TIMOTHY 1:13

Words of encouragement can be healing to our souls. The testimony of God's gospel and its transformative power in our lives is a balm to the weary heart. Our healing and hope can breathe healing and hope into others. Our stories of victory can impart courage to those fighting their own battles.

Take time to meditate on an encouraging word or testimony you've heard recently. If you have your own testimony to share, reach out to someone you know who may need to hear an encouraging word. Just as Solomon said in Proverbs 16:24, "Nothing is more appealing than speaking beautiful, life-giving words. For they release sweetness to our souls and inner healing to our spirits."

Anointed One, may my love for you continue to grow as I hear about how you are moving in others' lives. May it blossom in the light of your mercy in my own life. Your words are like honey, and I can't get enough.

Empowered by Grace

Timothy, my dear son, live your life empowered by God's free-flowing grace, which is your true strength, found in the anointing of Jesus and your union with him!

2 TIMOTHY 2:1

True strength isn't found in how self-sufficient we are. It's not in the diminishment of our needs. Having needs does not make us weak; it makes us human. Being able to do it all on our own may be idolized in our culture, but it is not actually a trait of the kingdom of God.

We rely on the grace of God to empower us in our weakness. Paul says in 2 Corinthians 12:10, "My weakness becomes a portal to God's power." We get to rely on the body of Christ, too, for support. When we name our needs with those we are in relationship with, we give them an opportunity to support us if they are able. This is also a picture of God's grace at work. May we be people who lean into the grace of God in every way we can.

Gracious God, thank you for your incomparable loving-kindness that brings me to life. You are my support and shield, and I am grateful for the opportunity to help and be helped by those in your family.

Deposits of Wisdom

All that you've learned from me, confirmed by the integrity of my life, deposit into faithful leaders who are competent to teach the congregations the same revelation.

2 TIMOTHY 2:2

When we take what we have learned through the years and deposit it into others who are looking to walk the same path, we partner with the expansion of possibility in the earth. When we sow seeds from our own orchard into the gardens of others, and they do the same for others after them, the possible effects are limitless.

Why would we hoard our knowledge for ourselves when we could sow into a greater legacy? Scarcity is not a mindset of the kingdom. There is more than enough room for all of us at the table. There is more than enough opportunity, more than enough time for each voice to be heard, more than enough resources to share with others. Let's live from the abundance of Christ and follow his generous lead.

Good God, I choose to live from a place of generosity rather than poverty. I won't hoard my wisdom, knowledge, or wealth. I will sow my first fruits into your kingdom and into those who have a hunger to do the same.

Worthy Focus

Make Jesus, the Anointed One, your focus in life and ministry. For he came to earth as the descendant of David and rose from the dead, according to the revelation of the gospel that God has given me.

2 TIMOTHY 2:8

Whether or not you find yourself in ministry, Jesus can be the focus of your life. You don't have to work for a church, volunteer for a non-profit, or call yourself a pastor in order to make an impact for Christ. When your life is centered around Christ, all that you do is worship. All that you offer him is pleasing.

Live a life of integrity, following the path of Christ's laid-down-love in the ins and outs of your day. Treat others with respect and kindness, offering compassion instead of judgment when others turn a cold shoulder. Be a safe harbor for those who would never step foot in a church. Whatever it is you do, make Jesus the focus and you can't go wrong.

Jesus, I center my life around you. Your fellowship is the most important relationship I have in life. There's nothing I want more than to know you, to honor you, and to be found in you in every area of my life.

Promote Encouragement

Be committed to teach the believers all these things when you are with them in the presence of the Lord. Instruct them to never be drawn into meaningless arguments, or tear each other down with useless words that only harm others.

2 TIMOTHY 2:14

It's safe to say that over the last few years, we have all been pulled into meaningless arguments at one point or another. The world is full of very loud and divided opinions. This is true in the church, as well. Let's make sure we keep first things first and follow the wisdom of God, as given through his Word.

Where we have used our words to tear others down, may we redirect our focus. We may need to ask for forgiveness. We may need to reconcile with those from whom we have distanced ourselves. We may need to forgive others. Instead of using words to get our own ideas across, let's use our words to uplift, encourage, and love one another well. What a difference it would make if we did.

Loving Lord, I know that there is so much mercy in your presence. There is so much grace and forgiveness. You don't use your Word to belittle others but to uplift them. I want to do the same. Your love is all that matters.

December

Holy Pursuit

Run as fast as you can from all the ambitions and lusts of youth; and chase after all that is pure. Whatever builds up your faith and deepens your love must become your holy pursuit. And live in peace with all those who worship our Lord Jesus with pure hearts.

2 TIMOTHY 2:22

How can we be prepared for every good work that God gives us to do? Not only by avoiding temptation but also by chasing after all that God's kingdom offers. Christ is the pure prize, and his life in us is more satisfying than the temporary pleasures that distract us from his love.

Whatever builds up our faith and whatever deepens our love, let that become our holy pursuit. David described the pure pleasure found in God's presence in Psalm 84. "How enriched are they who find their strength in the Lord; within their hearts are the highways of holiness…they grow stronger and stronger with every step forward" (vv. 5, 7). Let's walk the ancient path of holiness, leaning on God's strength as he leads us into his presence.

Glorious One, I choose to pursue you not out of obligation but out of desire. Your kindness is better than anything I've ever tasted. Build up my faith and deepen my love as I walk with you.

Fierce Days

> You need to be aware that in the final days
> the culture of society will become extremely fierce.
>
> 2 TIMOTHY 3:1

P aul goes on to describe the fierceness of culture by describing how people will become more self-centered and looking out only for themselves. Others will become obsessed with money. Pride and arrogance will run rampant. Ungratefulness and disconnectedness will increase.

This is not the whole of the story, though. There are also those who love goodness and kindness, who seek to share the mercy-kindness of God, and who live with integrity. We get to choose whom we will spend time around. When we choose to surround ourselves with those who care more about pleasing God than pleasing themselves, we choose wisely. The days are fierce, but the love of God cuts through with even more force. Let's align ourselves with the power of his resurrection life and remain faithful to his loyal love.

Mighty God, your love is more powerful than the grave, and it is more powerful than the wickedness in the world. I choose to follow your path of mercy, knowing that there is renewal, peace, and life in your presence. You are better than any self-serving dream I could ever achieve.

Advancing in Truth

> You must continue to advance in strength with the truth wrapped around your heart, being assured by God that he's the One who has truly taught you all these things.

2 TIMOTHY 3:14

If we live with the belief that God will spare us from trouble or persecution as we follow him, we will be ill-prepared for the unexpected upsets in this life. God did not guarantee us a pain-free life. He did not promise that if we follow him, others will love us. In fact, Jesus told his disciples in John 15:18, "Just remember, when the unbelieving world hates you, they first hated me."

This is why we must lean on God's grace to strengthen us as we continue to pursue his love. With the truth of Christ wrapped around our hearts, even when others abandon us, we remain rooted in purpose. God will never forsake us. The path of mercy can feel lonely at times. But we are never truly alone. Every sacrifice we make in loyal love will be worth it in the end.

Jesus, thank you for the reminder that not being liked is not the same thing as falling out of your favor. I stand on the solid foundation of your grace, and I follow you, no matter what. Be near, Lord.

Sacred Lessons

Remember what you were taught from your childhood from the Holy Scrolls which can impart to you wisdom to experience everlasting life through the faith of Jesus, the Anointed One.

2 TIMOTHY 3:15

Not all of us were taught the Scriptures as children. This does not disqualify anyone from the fullness we find in Christ. We have been welcomed into the family of God with open arms, and no one is lesser for their lack of exposure to his Word.

Whatever inspires mercy, joy, peace, patience, and the other fruits of the Spirit are tools of God's wisdom in this world. There are keys to Christ's kingdom in the Scriptures, and there is so much wisdom to inspire us to live with faith in the written testimony of God's lovers throughout history. Let's not forget the lessons we learned when we were younger; we can incorporate them into our lived experience now.

Holy One, thank you for the sacred lessons I have learned in my life. Thank you for the lessons that I have yet to learn. Bring to mind the power of your gospel and how it reached me at first. Teach me with the wisdom of your Word.

Inspired Scripture

God has transmitted his very substance into every Scripture, for it is
God-breathed. It will empower you by its instruction and correction,
giving you the strength to take the right direction and lead you deeper
into the path of godliness.

2 TIMOTHY 3:16

God's nature is embedded in the Holy Scriptures. In the Old
Testament, we see how gracious and merciful he was to his
people throughout their journey. Every time they returned to him
in repentance, he forgave their sins and restored them. He was
faithful to the promises he spoke over them. He supernaturally
provided for them. He appeared as a cloud by day and a pillar of
fire by night when the Israelites wandered in the desert. He never
left them.

Do you need fresh perspective today of who God is? Do you
need direction? Are you simply looking for encouragement? Are
you looking to deepen your faith? Whatever it is that you are
looking for today, spend some time in the Word of God. May the
Spirit breathe his revelation knowledge into your heart and mind
and bring you deeper understanding. He is faithful to be reveal
himself when you look for him.

*Great God, I won't neglect your Scriptures today. Deepen my
reverence for you as I encounter your incomparable character in the
pages of your Word. Speak to me; I am listening.*

Stand on Scripture

Proclaim the Word of God and stand upon it no matter what! Rise
to the occasion and preach when it is convenient and when it is not.
Preach in the full expression of the Holy Spirit—with wisdom and
patience as you instruct and teach the people.

2 TIMOTHY 4:2

Timothy was called by God to be a preacher and leader of the
early church. Though we are not all called to be teachers and
preachers, we are all living reflections of God's redemptive power.
Whatever our gift is, whatever it is that God has placed within us,
we must be ready to practice it both in and out of season—when
it is convenient and when it is not.

When we stand upon the foundation of God's Word, no
matter what circumstances may come—storms, sickness, trials,
or tremendous favor—we will not be moved from the purposes of
God in our lives. Let's rise to the occasion to share what God has
done, in the full expression of his Spirit, through the gifts we have
to offer.

*Living God, I trust that your Word is living and active in this world
as well as in my life. I won't neglect the gifts that you have place
within me. I cultivate them and use them for your glory.*

Heart Full of Faith

I have fought an excellent fight.
I have finished my full course with all my might
and I've kept my heart full of faith.

2 TIMOTHY 4:7

P aul was nearing the end of his life, and he knew it. He had traveled extensively sharing the good news of the gospel of Christ. He had helped found and disciple new churches in various regions. He was a missionary and an apostle. He had been persecuted for proclaiming his faith, and he was imprisoned for it. Ultimately, he would die for it.

May we live with hearts full of faith, focused energy on the gospel of Christ and its power to save, transform, and liberate. Let's share freely the gifts we have received in faith. Let's live open-hearted and generous lives. Let's pour out the love and mercy of God in practical ways. Let's live for a larger purpose than to please ourselves. In all things, no matter what the course of our lives looks like, let's keep our hearts full of faith.

Jesus, I want to follow your example like Paul did. Keep my heart full of faith as I lean on your Spirit's power to save, redeem, and restore. You are the passion of my life.

Never Alone

In spite of this, my Lord himself stood with me, empowering me
to complete my ministry of preaching to all the non-Jewish nations
so they all could hear the message and be delivered from the mouth
of the lion!

2 TIMOTHY 4:17

Even when Paul's companions abandoned him, the Lord never did. In the same way, no matter how alone we may feel, the Spirit of God never abandons us. He is with us. He wraps around us with the loyal love of his presence. Psalm 144:2 says, "He's my shelter of love and my fortress of faith, who wraps himself around me as a secure shield."

Whatever we are facing, God does not leave us to walk into it alone. He wraps himself around us as a shield. He is our source of strength and our defender. His presence is ever so near, as Paul describes in 1 Corinthians 6:19: "The gift of God, the Holy Spirit, lives inside your sanctuary." That is, the sanctuary of our souls. We are never alone with the Spirit of God dwelling within.

Holy Spirit, thank you for making your home within me. You are my hope, my strength, and my peace. Give me courage to face whatever comes with your help. Thank you.

Glory to God

My Lord will continue to deliver me from every form of evil
and give me life in his heavenly kingdom. May all the glory
go to him alone for all the ages of eternity!

2 TIMOTHY 4:18

Paul's ultimate hope was in Christ and the eternal life he would share in his kingdom. The Lord was faithful to deliver Paul from many evils, not the least of which was a prison sentence. However, Paul's ultimate hope of deliverance was not from human hands but from the confines of this world. Earlier in this chapter, he admitted that he was ready to die for his faith and that the time was approaching when he would.

We will not be physically delivered from every trouble that comes our way, and yet that does not reflect on God's faithfulness. Let us understand what our true calling is, where our true hope lies, and what is our purpose in this life. May God receive glory through our surrendered lives no matter what it looks like. Let's trust him, for he is good and will not fail to give us life in his heavenly kingdom.

King of heaven, this life is but a short journey on the way to eternity. I want to keep my eyes focused on you, on your unrelenting love, and the all-surpassing goodness of knowing you. Be glorified.

Eternal Hope

I'm writing to you to further the faith of God's chosen ones and lead
them to the full knowledge of the truth that leads to godliness,
which rests on the hope of eternal life.

TITUS 1:1–2

I f all we had was this life, with no hope for anything after, how
differently would we live? Would it feel meaningless, or would
we still give ourselves to generous love, mercy, and justice? In
Christ, we have an eternal hope that never fades. And "faith
brings our hopes into reality and becomes the foundation needed
to acquire the things we long for" (Hebrews 11:1).

God is not a liar. He keeps every promise he made. His vows,
once spoken, cannot be broken. He will always act in faithfulness,
and he won't ever change his nature. He is greater than we can
imagine, being fully just and also full of unending mercy. Let's
give our lives to knowing him, to living worthy of the calling. Let's
be like him, for any act of loving-kindness sows into the realm
of his kingdom. He is worthy of our faith, our hope, and our
deference.

*Eternal King, there was no one before you, and no one will come after
you. Reveal the wonders of your love to me in new ways today as I
give my energy, focus, and attention to knowing and living for you.*

Lovers of Goodness

Instead he should be one who is known for his hospitality
and a lover of goodness. He should be recognized
as one who is fair-minded, pure-hearted, and self-controlled.

TITUS 1:8

As living reflections of God's love, we should endeavor to live as lovers of his goodness. For anyone to be entrusted with leadership in the church or over other believers, they should be known for their hospitality also. Why is this important? Those who are known for their hospitality do not show favoritism. They are welcoming to all. This means that different kinds of people should feel comfortable going to them with concerns.

No matter if we lead a small group or a large ministry, whether we meet one-on-one or with many, may we be people who are known for our openheartedness. Let's be lovers of goodness, promoting the kingdom of Christ through our lifestyles and our interactions with others. This is a worthy pursuit.

Good Father, you are so full of mercy, and you welcome all who turn to you. I want to live out that same kindness in my own life. Give me your compassion and cultivate my character with your gracious help.

Pure Hearts

It's true that all is pure to those who have pure hearts,
but to the corrupt unbelievers nothing is pure.

TITUS 1:15

I f we claim to know God but we deny him by our actions, then our faith means nothing. True faith is lived out. Our values and beliefs inform our lifestyles. God is gracious, and he offers help to those who lean on him for understanding. He transforms us in the liquid mercy of his presence. As we gaze upon him, yielding our hearts to him, he purifies our hearts and covers us with his righteousness.

No one is a lost cause. Paul has advice for those who want to walk in the ways of God in Romans 12:2. He says, "Stop imitating the ideals and opinions of the culture around you…be inwardly transformed by the Holy Spirit through a total reformation of how you think." The Holy Spirit transforms us from the inside out, and when we become learners of the culture of his kingdom, we adopt his ways and leave popular opinion behind.

Spirit, thank you for the power of your work in my heart and life. I give myself to learning the ways of your kingdom and applying them in my life. I want to be known as yours. Purify my heart in your mercy.

Godly Qualities

Lead the male elders into disciplined lives full of dignity and self-control.
Urge them to have a solid faith, generous love, and patient endurance.

TITUS 2:2

A life of discipline may not sound exciting to us. No one achieves anything important without some level of sacrifice. We know that boundaries open us up to focus and protect what is important as much as they cut excess out. Discipline that leads to self-control is godly. When it leads to dignity, it is honorable.

Hebrews 12:11 says, "All discipline seems to be painful at the time, yet later it will produce a transformation of character, bringing a harvest of righteousness and peace to those who yield to it." Will we submit to the process of disciplining ourselves so that we reap the reward? Let's continue to build our lives on the solid foundation of our faith, generously living out the love of the Lord and patiently enduring all that comes.

Merciful God, I don't despise your correction in my life, nor will I avoid building practices of righteousness into my life. I want my whole life to reflect the power of your mercy. I choose to walk in your ways.

Be the Example

Above all, set yourself apart as a model of a life nobly lived.
With dignity, demonstrate integrity in all that you teach.

TITUS 2:7

We can only reflect that which we know. If we want to live as models of Christ's love, then we need to know its depth. Our lives become beacons of our beliefs, and our beliefs are formed in the transformation of God's living Word at work within us. When we give our time and attention to studying the Word of God, we are able to apply its power to our lives.

Why would we try to teach something that we know nothing of? Trustworthy teaching is found in those who have tried and tested integrity. We should not teach impulsively from our own opinion, for this will surely lead to arguments and divisions. Experts in specified fields spend time doing extensive research, as well as applying it with experience. If we want to be experts in Christ and his gospel, then we will do the same.

Lord Jesus, I don't venture to be an expert in your kingdom though I want to know you more. I know this takes time, attention, and application. As I seek you, reveal yourself through your Word, the fellowship of your Spirit, and your revelation-knowledge.

Sound Message

Bring a clear, wholesome message that cannot be condemned, and then your critics will be embarrassed, with nothing bad to say about us.

TITUS 2:8

The preaching of the Word of God should be based in the gospel of Christ. It should be clear, not confusing, and full of the fruit of God's Spirit. It should not be biased or filled with personal opinion. The message of the gospel in simplest form is the power of the death, resurrection, and lordship of Jesus Christ. In his mercy, we put our faith in Christ and share in his resurrection life.

May we come back to the foundation of the simplicity of the gospel whenever we get distracted by arguments among believers. Let's focus our attention on the power of Christ's sacrifice and the new life he offers us through his Spirit. Let's lay down the divisive opinions that spin us in circles and push us further from unity with one another. Let's let love cover our offense. Let's look to Christ and uphold his message and ministry as our standard.

Jesus Christ, you are the only Savior. Your perfect love covers the error of my ways. I want to promote peace and true unity in your love both in what I say and how I live my life.

Personified Grace

God's marvelous grace has manifested in person, bringing salvation for everyone. This same grace teaches us how to live each day as we turn our backs on ungodliness and indulgent lifestyles, and it equips us to live self-controlled, upright, godly lives in this present age.

TITUS 2:11–12

God's kindness and love are extended to us through his grace. Every moment it is available, making us worthy of Christ's acceptance. It is unconditional, unmerited, and completely indescribable favor from our Lord.

The grace of God empowers us to live with self-control, upright in our behavior, and godly before God's eyes. The outflow of our behavior reflects the source of our strength. There is wisdom to instruct us, power to turn from the destructive patterns of this world, and an endless source of living love to refresh, renew, and supply us with more to offer others. We can never earn this grace, but there is no need. We turn to Christ, and he offers us all that we could ever require.

Gracious Jesus, thank you for the abundance of kindness and love I find in you. I give up trying to earn your favor, and instead I simply receive the generous grace you offer. Thank you.

Waiting in Anticipation

We continue to wait for the fulfillment of our hope in the dawning splendor of the glory of our great God and Savior, Jesus, the Anointed One.

TITUS 2:13

As we wait for the fulfillment of our blessed hope and the glorious appearing of Christ, may we keep the anticipation burning within our hearts. Have we forgotten the promise of his coming? In this season, there are reminders of how Jesus took on flesh and came as a baby born thousands of years ago. May we take the opportunity of this celebration season to prepare our hearts for his return.

Through the glorious appearing of Christ as a baby, a wonderful hope was brought into the world. Through the grace of God through his Spirit, we have hope for the manifestation of Christ's reappearance. May we cultivate the desire of the fullness of his presence through fellowship with his Spirit. He will come again, and we will see and know him even as surely as we are seen and known by him.

Jesus, I long for your return and for the fullness of your kingdom to be established on earth as it is in heaven. Awaken my hope in the grace of your Spirit's presence.

Confront the Truth

So preach these truths and exhort others to follow them.
Be willing to expose sin in order to bring correction with
full authority, without being intimidated by anyone.

TITUS 2:15

In order to bring correction, we have to be able to confront the truth. We can't avoid hard realities in the name of love. We must be willing to first recognize the reality of the situation and then bring correction. Love does not sweep things under the rug. It lays it all out in the open.

If we are not willing to expose sin for what it is, those who prey on the vulnerable will be able to keep hurting people in the shadows. Accountability is important, especially for those in a place of power. God will not be mocked, and what we sow, we will reap. May we be filled with the Spirit who gives us mighty power to face the truth head on. Mercy saves, but let's not forget that mercy also confronts and corrects in loving truth.

God who sees, nothing escapes your sight. You see everything done in the open and in secret. May I never shrink back from confronting harsh truths for fear of the consequences. Your grace is my strength.

Considerate of Differences

Remind them to never tear down anyone with their words
or quarrel, but instead be considerate, humble,
and courteous to everyone.

TITUS 3:2

D o we value our similarities over our call to love one
another? When we look at creation, we see a wonderful
diversity of beauty. It would be preposterous for us to lament that
a rock was not a seashell or that a snail wasn't an elephant. Every
creature has value in the earth, and each of us has value in the
kingdom of God.

May we pursue peace by building each other up in love. This
does not mean that we need to all look the same, dress the same,
or talk the same. Agreement on all things isn't possible. May we
learn to delight in each other's differences, knowing that safety
and connection doesn't come from how alike we are but how
much we love each other.

*Loving Lord, I want to reflect your liberating love in my
relationships. May I allow others to be who they are and not who I
think they should be. Thank you that this is the freedom you give in
your mercy.*

Extraordinary Mercy

When the extraordinary compassion of God our Savior and his overpowering love suddenly appeared in person, as the brightness of a dawning day, he came to save us. Not because of any virtuous deed that we have done but only because of his extravagant mercy.

TITUS 3:4–5

What extraordinary mercy is displayed in Christ's coming. God, moved by immense love, appeared in person as a baby. The prophet Isaiah foretold that day saying, "A child has been born for us; a son has been given to us…his name will be: The Wonderful One…The Prince of Peace!" (9:6). Christ came in human form, laying aside his divinity for a time. He would bring light to the world in a time of darkness.

Jesus Christ is the light of the world still. He shines like the brightness of a dawning day. In John 8:12, Jesus said, "I am light to the world, and those who embrace me will experience life-giving light, and they will never walk in darkness." The life-giving light of Christ is alive within us, overpowering the darkness of sin and death. What a wonderful Savior he is!

Messiah, the extraordinary compassion that you displayed in laying down your deity and taking on the frailty of humanity is more than I can fathom. Thank you for your saving grace and for your mighty mercy.

Refreshing Waters

He saved us, resurrecting us through the washing of rebirth.
We are made completely new by the Holy Spirit, whom he
splashed over us richly by Jesus, the Messiah, our Life Giver.

TITUS 3:6

Our salvation is not only for a far-off day when we pass from this life to the next. Christ makes us new now in the resurrection power of his life within us. Renewal is ours now through the Spirit. As we put our faith in him and yield our hearts to him, he loves us to life in his mercy.

There is the power to transform our hearts and minds alive within us. Second Corinthians 5:17 says, "If anyone is enfolded into Christ, he has become an entirely new person. All that is related to the old order has vanished. Behold, everything is fresh and new." We are washed in the refreshing waters of his Spirit's presence. What a beautiful mystery is the life of Christ within us.

Life Giver, thank you for making me completely new in you. You have removed the stain of my guilt and shame, and you have purified my heart in your love. What glorious mercy you pour out.

Waterfalls of Hope

So as a gift of his love, and since we are faultless—
innocent before his face—we can now become heirs of all things,
all because of an overflowing hope of eternal life.

TITUS 3:7

In the mercy-tide of Christ's salvation, we are completely pure before God the Father. He sees us through the lens of Christ's innocence. In Christ, we are then qualified to share in the treasures of his kingdom. Romans 8:17 says it this way, "Since we are joined to Christ, we also inherit all that he is and all that he has."

Our hopes are firmly planted in the realm of his eternal kingdom where we will dwell with him. We have a glimpse of what it will be like in Revelation 22:5: "Night will be no more. They will never need the light of the sun or a lamp, because the Lord God will shine on them. And they will reign as kings forever and ever!" We will reign with Christ. What a glorious hope!

Christ, fill my heart with the hope of your eternal kingdom that knows no end. Where change forces me to see as many ends as I do beginnings in this life, I know that there is a greater reality with you. Thank you.

Faithful Message

I want you to especially emphasize these truths, so that those who
believe in God will be careful to devote themselves to doing good works.
It is always beautiful and profitable for believers to do good works.

When we live for God, with our faith fueling our choices
and lifestyles, we express the beliefs of our hearts in the
actions of our hands. As Paul says here, "It is always beautiful and
profitable for believers to do good works." Let's not forget how
important this is.

We can find this echoed in other parts of Scripture. James
says that when our actions cooperate with our faith, by our action
faith finds its full expression (2:22). When we are devoted to God,
we will also be devoted to good works. Our actions will express
the kingdom values that we believe as we partner with his purposes on this earth. There is always more room to grow, so let's
not let shame hold us back. Let's look to what is ours to do now.

*Faithful One, you move in mercy in tangible ways, and I will do the
same. I won't claim to simply know your love, but I will live it out in
practical acts of kindness and compassion.*

Bring It Back to Christ

Avoid useless controversies, genealogies, pointless quarrels,
and arguments over the law, which will get you nowhere.

TITUS 3:9

Where is our focus today? As we prepare our hearts to celebrate the first coming of Christ, perhaps we have already laid aside useless controversies and pointless quarrels. Perhaps in the "spirit of the season" we have chosen instead to extend kindness and compassion, looking for ways to brighten others' days.

Let's carry that same energy into every season. It is too easy to get distracted by arguments that lead nowhere. We don't have to convince each other of our opinions. The call is always first and foremost to love one another, and love is best expressed in practical ways. May Christ be our focus throughout the year, as much as he is this week. He is worthy of our celebration, and his love is always overflowing—a never-ending source to draw from.

Christ Jesus, thank you for the simplicity of this season and the ability to focus on you. Help me carry that with me all the time, choosing love over control, kindness over judgment, and mercy over offense.

Beautiful Fruit

Encourage the believers to be passionately devoted to beautiful works of righteousness by meeting the urgent needs of others and not be unfruitful.

TITUS 3:14

Are we devoted to works of righteousness as much as we claim to be devoted to the Lord? First John 3:18 says, "Our love can't be an abstract theory we only talk about, but a way of life demonstrated through our loving deeds." The fruit of the Spirit is not proven in our theories of God, but in the way our love is lived out—how we are known to others.

May we be as passionate about doing good deeds as we are about worshiping the Lord with our words. We don't earn God's love by doing good; we pour out the overflow of what he is already pouring into us. This is more practical than it sounds. Love propels us to be kind, to look for ways to help others, and to produce good fruit.

Great God, when I think of your love, the proof is not in the feeling but in your actions. You took our salvation upon yourself, doing all the work and offering free grace. I know that as I live for you, my actions reflect your mercy in real ways.

Faithful to Love

I am always thankful to my God as I remember you in my prayers because I'm hearing reports about your faith in the Lord Jesus and how much love you have for all his holy followers.

PHILEMON 1:4–5

How we treat others will always be a reflection of our hearts. The love of Christ pours out in tangible ways as we partner with his purposes. Philemon was known for his faith and love, and Paul recognizes this in his letter. Do our interactions with others leave a lasting impact for the gospel of Christ? May our choices bring glory to God and gratitude to others.

How can we choose to use our influence for the Lord? Let's start from a place of surrendered love in our fellowship with the Spirit. Spending time in his presence, let's offer him the adoration of our hearts through worship, the openness of our lives through prayer, and the willingness of our partnership through our devotion throughout our day.

Father, thank you for the gift of your Son and for the fellowship of your Spirit. I have put all my trust in you, and I long to reveal your love through the relationships I have. May you be glorified in my life.

Shared Faith

I pray for you that the faith we share may effectively deepen your understanding of every good thing that belongs to you in Christ.

PHILEMON 1:6

There is a never-ending opportunity to grow in and deepen our understanding of God through our faith. When we spend time with others who share this faith, we are able to encourage and sharpen one another. None of us has full revelation of Christ. We all see in part and know in part. As we share with each other the revelations and testimonies of his work in our lives, we also share in that deepening understanding.

We can also deepen our experience of faith through sharing it with those who do not have a relationship with the Lord. As we relate what God has done for us, how he has transformed our lives through the glorious goodness of his gospel, our own hearts grow the grace of our lived testimony.

Gracious One, may my understanding grow stronger in the sharing of my faith with others. I want to know you more, to reveal your goodness to others, and to walk in the fullness of all that you offer.

Love's Impact

> Your love has impacted me and brings me great joy and
> encouragement, for the hearts of the believers have been
> greatly refreshed through you, dear brother.
>
> PHILEMON 1:7

We all have people in our lives who have impacted us through their lived-out love. There is so much joy in the refreshing company of a good and trusted friend. Let's take the time to consider all the encouragers in our lives. Who has made a lasting impact on our lives through their faithful support? Who has been like a refreshing river in a dry desert to our souls?

Let's take this opportunity to follow the example of Paul and express our gratitude. Whether we do it in person, in writing, or in another creative way, let's reach out and thank those pillars in our lives. Love leaves an imprint on us, and it has the possibility to refresh us anew as we consider their kindness.

Joyful Jesus, you are full of love that brings hope, joy, and encouragement. Thank you for those in my life who have been your living example in my life. I hope that others may be able to say the same of me.

From Slave to Brother

Welcome him no longer as a slave, but more than that, as a dearly loved brother. He is that to me especially, and how much more so to you, both humanly speaking and in the Lord.

PHILEMON 1:16

Paul's appeal to Philemon was significant. This letter was to accompany a former fugitive slave back to Philemon's household. Paul asked Philemon to restore him to his household, not as a slave but as a brother in Christ. This was no small ask. And yet it is filled with the redemptive mercy of God through Jesus.

Christ has offered us full restoration in his mercy and has forgiven all our offenses. May we be like him in our own relationships. When others humble themselves, seeking forgiveness, may we hear them out with open hearts. We are brothers and sisters, so let's not hold our old power dynamics over each other.

Redeemer, you are incredibly rich in mercy, and you won't ever run out of grace. I lean on this love to line my heart in my relationships. May I be quick to forgive as you are, God.

In the Same Way

If you consider me your friend and partner,
accept him the same way you would accept me.

PHILEMON 1:17

Paul asked Philemon to show mercy to Onesimus, accepting him as he would Paul himself. When we advocate for others, it is not without our own personal investment. In the next verse, Paul continued, "If he has stolen anything from you or owes you anything, just place it on my account." Paul was willing to vouch for the transformation in Onesimus' life with his own resources.

Restoration is a worthy pursuit. Redemption is the work of the gospel's power in our lives. Forgiveness is a key element to unity and reconciliation. In Christ, there is enough love to cover all our sin; there is also enough forgiveness to reconcile with those who have wounded us. May we be people who do the worthwhile and hard work of forgiveness, for in Christ, we have all been reconciled by mercy.

Merciful Jesus, thank you for the forgiveness you so freely offer all who come to you in repentance. I know that it is better to forgive than to live in a walled fortress of self-protection and bitterness. I choose your way over my own. Spirit, help me.

Benediction

May the unconditional love of the Lord Jesus,
the Anointed One, be with your spirit!

When we are wrapped in Christ, we are covered in his love. There is more than enough mercy for every circumstance we face. There is plentiful grace in his presence. We are never without his help, and we need never rely on our own strength to power through.

May the overpowering love of God's presence overwhelm your senses and fill you with peace as you follow Christ's steps for your life. May you know the surpassing goodness of his leadership, the wonderful wisdom of his perspective, and the power of his resurrection life in every season. Walk in the light of his presence, for he is your Savior and has everything you need.

Jesus Christ, you are the light of my life, and your love is the fire that burns in my soul. Fill me with more of your grace today as I look to you. Lead me on, for you are my true hope, my resting place, and my shield. I love you.

About the Author

Brian Simmons is the lead translator of The Passion Translation®. The Passion Translation (TPT) is a heart-level translation that uses Hebrew, Greek, and Aramaic manuscripts to express God's fiery heart of love to this generation, merging the emotion and life-changing truth of God's Word. The hope for TPT is to trigger inside every reader an overwhelming response to the truth of the Bible and to reveal the deep mysteries of the Scriptures in the love language of God, the language of the heart. Brian is currently translating the Old Testament.

After a dramatic conversion to Christ in 1971, Brian and his wife, Candice, answered the call of God to leave everything behind and become missionaries to unreached peoples. Taking their three children to the tropical rain forest of Central America, they planted churches for many years with the Paya-Kuna people group. Brian established leadership for the churches that Jesus birthed and, having been trained in linguistics and Bible translation principles, assisted with the translation of the Paya-Kuna New Testament.

After their ministry overseas, Brian and Candice returned to North America, where Brian began to passionately work toward helping people encounter the risen Christ. He and his wife planted numerous ministries, including a dynamic church in New England (US). They also established

Passion & Fire Ministries, under which they travel full time as Bible teachers in service of local churches throughout the world.

Brian is the author of numerous books, Bible studies, and devotionals that help readers encounter God's heart and experience a deeper revelation of God as our Bridegroom-King, including *Throne Room Prayer*, *The Sacred Journey*, *Prayers on Fire*, *The Divine Romance*, and *The Vision*.

Brian and Candice have been married since 1971 and have three children as well as precious grandchildren and great-grandchildren. Their passion is to live as loving examples of a spiritual father and mother to this generation.